William Albert Samuel Hewins

English Trade and Finance

17th Century

William Albert Samuel Hewins

English Trade and Finance
17th Century

ISBN/EAN: 9783744662413

Printed in Europe, USA, Canada, Australia, Japan

Cover: Foto ©Suzi / pixelio.de

More available books at **www.hansebooks.com**

NANCE

TURY

BY

W. A. S. HEWI

Late Scholar of Pembroke Co
University Extension Lecturer on
Late Lecturer to the Toynbee Trust; some
Economy at University Colle

Methuen & Co.

18, BURY STREET, LONDON, W.C.

1892

Richard Clay & Sons, Limited,
London & Bungay.

PREFACE.

THE following chapters were the subject-matter of lectures which formed part of a course or courses on economic history, and were delivered at Oxford during the Summer Meetings of 1889 and 1890, in various University Extension centres in the north of England, and at University College, Bristol. The object I have kept in view in preparing the book for the press has been, not to supply an exhaustive sketch of the economic activities of the period dealt with, but to supplement, from contemporary authorities, the larger works which can be obtained from the Travelling Library, and which are usually read by the students. It may be pointed out that these students are men and women of all ages and of various attainments. A lecturer on economics usually finds that his audience, in a manufacturing town, consists of a few employers of labour and other business men, clerks, artisans, co-operators and trade unionists, a small number of women of the middle and working-classes, and a sprinkling of High School and elementary teachers.

In the Introduction I have pointed out the general character of the economic writings of the seventeenth century, and the influence of the discussion of the difficulties or the grievances of that period on the growth of the theory of the balance of trade. I have not considered it necessary, however, to discuss the writers—*e. g.*, Nicholas Barbon, Sir Dudley North, Simon Clement, and Locke—whose grasp of certain fundamental conceptions in economic science was clearer than that of the exponents of the theory of the balance of trade, though certainly three out of the four writers mentioned were infected with the errors of the mercantile system. Thomas Milles' canons of taxation appear to have been overlooked by writers on this subject. The quotation on p. xviii on the grievances of the merchants is from a MS. note by the author in the Bodleian copy of the "Custumer's Apology." The Court Minutes of the East India Company (Cal. S. P. Colonial) make clear Thomas Mun's share in developing the theory of the Balance of Trade.

In the chapter on the Commercial Treaties I have illustrated the changes in public opinion on commercial subjects during the eighteenth century. The controversy about the Free Trade clauses of the Treaty of Utrecht had important results, and I have quoted at length a passage from *Mercator* which illustrates the advanced views advocated by Defoe and other writers in that series of papers.

The hasty manner in which the theory of evolution has been applied in economic history has frequently led writers on this subject too readily to attribute beneficial results to the combinations of the sixteenth and seventeenth centuries. It is probable that more stress should be laid on the hostility to the various forms of monopoly which are found during that period. The number and the resources of those who had no such special privileges must be important elements when we are forming an opinion of the success or failure of these methods of regulating industry and commerce. It is noteworthy that the House of Commons on several occasions showed itself more favourable than the commercial classes to free enterprise. The early appeals to natural right are also remarkable. To illustrate the policy of the Trading Companies, I have given a general sketch of their constitution and objects, and a detailed account of some incidents in the history of four of these associations.

Further investigation confirms on the whole the late Professor Thorold Rogers' views of the depressed and unhappy condition of the working-classes during the seventeenth century, and, particularly, the evil effects of the Statute of Apprenticeship on the wages of artisans and agricultural labourers. But he insisted too much upon the character of that statute as a new departure, and he was mistaken in the motives he ascribed to the Government and to those who administered the law. Of the Wages Assessments, mentioned on page 82, he printed twelve in his *Agriculture and Prices* (vols. iv. and vi.). He also gave particulars of a Lancashire Assessment (1725) in *Work and Wages*. But he overlooked four important assessments noticed in Hamilton's *Quarter Sessions from Elizabeth to Anne*. These were kindly pointed out to me by Mr. C. H. Firth, who also drew my attention to three others—two in the Belvoir Papers and one in *Mercurius Politicus*. Dr. Cox has printed two valuable Derbyshire assessments in his *Derbyshire Annals*, and allusion is made to another in the *Middlesex County Records*, edited by J. C. Jeaffreson. The Gloucestershire assessment, printed at the end of this book, comes from *A State of the Case, etc., of the late Commotions* (1757). I hope shortly to print some more documents of the same kind, for which I am indebted to the Mayor and the Town Clerk of Colchester, and other sources. I have ventured to illustrate the life of a craftsman in the seventeenth century by that of a master workman in one of the Staffordshire domestic industries before they were directly affected by the introduction of machinery. The history of the family and descendants of a tenant-farmer has also been found useful as an illustration of the effect, on class distinctions, of the modern system of industry. The remarks on the condition of the workers in the nail trade and kindred trades are based on the recollections of many visits, some years ago, to the nailing districts, and investigation in the year 1887, corrected and extended by more recent inquiry, the blue-books bearing on the subject, and frequent residence in the district where the nut and bolt trade is chiefly carried on.

I have given one instance of the generous manner in which Mr. C. H. Firth has pointed out to me sources of information on the economic history of the seventeenth century. This, however, is only one out of the many suggestions for which I am indebted to him during the progress of this book.

W. A. S. Hewins.

18, *Museum Road, Oxford,*
April 30*th*, 1892.

INTRODUCTION.

WHATEVER delusions might lead astray the merchant of the seventeenth century when he published a pamphlet on some burning controversy of the day, he was not mistaken, in ordinary life, as to the nature of his wealth. He never for one moment supposed that it began and ended with the coin or bullion in his possession. He included the goods in his warehouse, the coins in his strong box, the debts due to him, his houses and lands, and the sum standing to his credit perhaps in the bank at Amsterdam or with some London goldsmith. His business was conducted on methods which would be quite intelligible to a merchant of the present day, for they were but those now in vogue imperfectly developed. He had waste-book, journal, and ledger, and balanced his accounts in a manner he had learnt from Italians or Dutchmen, and which we have learnt from him. He had excellent text-books on the subject, from those of Hugh Oldcastle, James Peel, and John Mellis at the end of the sixteenth century, to those of John Collins and Alex. Liset at the end of the seventeenth. If he were engaged in foreign trade, his factors and agents might be found in the great centres of European commerce, such as Antwerp, Amsterdam, Hamburg, Lisbon, Bourdeaux, and Rouen; while he would join in partnership with Dutchmen or Portuguese, if by that means he could facilitate his business arrangements or increase his profits. The merchant's education was intensely utilitarian, and apprenticeship supplied what our schemes of technical and commercial instruction taken alone can never supply. In this way he mastered the subjects, a clear knowledge of which was essential to the trader of the seventeenth century. In addition to the routine of business, he became acquainted by sight and touch with the commodities of the trading countries, and frequently with the conditions under which they were produced. He knew the various coinages of the European states, their financial systems, and their widely differing trading customs; and whether monopolist or free-trader, it was necessary for him to know their commercial laws and the powers and jurisdiction of their courts.

Thus equipped, he pursued in the manner then possible objects which in all ages appeal to men. The desire to make provision for his family or to live in ease and comfort, the ambition to rise to a prominent position in the municipality or the state, and the numerous other motives which are grouped together under the one phrase, desire of wealth, prompted the adoption of certain means of achieving those objects, which are as intelligible and as capable of scientific treatment as the social phenomena of our own time. The merchant of the seventeenth century was not less self-interested than his modern successor; indeed, if the dramatists are to be trusted, the average man of commerce during that period would have well-deserved the severe epithets which may be found in the anti-capitalist literature of to-day. We need not believe that there was

> "no religion, nor virtue
> But in abundance, and no vice but want;"

but the motives which some people apparently think came in with the spinning-jenny were as rife in the seventeenth century as they are now. The merchant then did not suppose, none but a philosopher ever did suppose, that if he unerringly followed his own interest the result would be the best possible for the community as a whole. On the contrary, there were instances, he believed, in which the individual's gain might be the commonwealth's loss, and he was fond of using this argument against a rival trader or an organization of which he was not a member. To buy as cheaply as possible and sell in the dearest market was one of the fundamental articles of his commercial creed, but numerous legal regulations were supposed to prevent one man from taking an unfair advantage of another, and the conception of intrinsic value was favourable to a higher standard of workmanship than is usual in our own day. Cautious and thrifty in his business, the ordinary merchant hesitated to embark in distant and uncertain undertakings, but this unwillingness could be overcome by the report of the large profits which the more adventurous reaped as the reward of their enterprise, and if he were put in the way of a lucrative commerce, or given a monopoly, he would "cleave like a clegg" to his privileges.

One of the most remarkable features of the latter part of the sixteenth and the seventeenth centuries was the frequency of attempts on the part of merchants or dealers to keep up or raise prices by combination, or by the formation of rings or corners. The study of the methods adopted is of great importance in tracing the growth of economic theory. Some account of these methods is given in the following pages. The most objectionable form which these combinations assumed was the patent or monopoly of the supply of some article of general consumption, such as salt, leather, coal, vinegar, glass, and starch. This it was easy enough for a court favourite to obtain in his own name, as a reward for real or alleged services, at a time when the need of protecting the interests of inventors, the financial difficulties of the Government, the industrial policy of the time, and other circumstances favoured the designs of monopolists. The hostile feeling of the general public against such abuses may be seen in the plays of the period, such as Ben Jonson's *The Devil is an Ass*, Randolph's *The Muses' Looking-Glass*, Brome's *Court Beggar*, *The Antipodes*, and *Holland's Leaguer;* in the debates in the House of Commons, and numerous contemporary pamphlets. A satirical pamphlet on the case of Alderman Abell and Richard Kilvert, who procured from Charles I. an exclusive patent for wine, well illustrates the methods by which such grants were sometimes obtained. Abell and Kilvert were prosecuted and heavily fined. On February 5th, 1641, a Bill was brought into the House of Commons dealing with their case, when it appeared they had in their hands "which they deceived the king of," £57,000 upon the wine license; the Vintners of London, £66,000; the wine merchants of Bristol, £1051; "all of which monies were ordered to be immediately raised on their lands and estates, and to be employed to the public use." In the pamphlet alluded to, Abell asks Kilvert how such a patent should be obtained, and he replies:—

"Marry, thus; we must first pretend both in the merchant and vintner some gross abuses, and these no meane ones either. And that the merchant shall pay to the king forty shillings for every tun ere he shall vent it to the vintner; in lieu of which, that the vintner may be no looser, he shall rayse the price also of his wines; upon all French wines a penny in the quart; upon all Spanish wines twopence in the quart; it is no matter how the subject suffers, so we get and gaine by it. Now to cover this our craft, (I will not say coinage,) because all things of the like nature carry a pretence for the king's profit, so we will allow him a competent proportion of forty thousand pounds per annum; when, the power of the patent being punctually executed, it will yield double at least, if not treble that sume, and returne it into the coffers of the undertakers."

The monopolies were not all as objectionable as the wine licence of Abell and Kilvert, but the evils which they entailed on large classes of traders and consumers, and analogous abuses in connection with the great trading companies, caused many attempts to remove the restrictions which were afterwards condemned in the *Wealth of Nations*. We must not expect to find, in the seventeenth century, the objections to these combinations based on the results of careful economic research. At the root of the opposition to monopolies and trading companies there seems to have been a strong feeling that every Englishman had a "natural right" to trade as he liked, provided he did not interfere with the liberty of others. Cecil, while defending Elizabeth's grants in the Parliament of 1601, condemned as "misdoers and wilful and wicked offenders" those who would "take from the subject his birthright"; and the opponents of the trading companies in 1604 appealed to the "natural right and liberty of the subjects of England" in support of two free trade bills. The Levellers, later on, gave a far more extended meaning to the phrase, and demanded universal suffrage and other measures as the natural right of all men.

The struggle of the Trading Companies with the outsiders began almost with their formation. Historical writers usually attribute the growth of English foreign trade during the sixteenth and the seventeenth centuries to the fostering care of these associations, but the evidence which we have of the way in which they secured and tried to maintain their monopoly does not point to such a conclusion. The political and social condition of the countries to which they traded, and the governmental functions which they had to discharge, made some organization necessary for the protection of property and the redress of grievances. No reasonable person would have objected to the regulation of trade by organizations to which admission was easy, which gave room for the adaptation of their rules to local needs, and which included all who desired to join. The Free Trade Bills of 1604, which passed the Commons with scarcely any opposition, would have secured these objects. A similar measure in 1497, when the Merchant Adventurers' Company alone had to be dealt with, would have satisfied all except the "London Fellowship," which for several years had been pursuing a monopolizing policy. The Government indeed reduced the fees, which that fellowship had raised from 6*s.* 8*d.* to £40 and claimed from all traders, to £6 13*s.* 4*d.*; but virtually legalized their exactions, and a few years later they received their charter. From that time onwards the privileges of the Merchant Adventurers were regarded as a grievance by a large section of the commercial world. It is sometimes urged that under free enterprise merchants would not have undertaken the risks of trading to distant places, that in fact such monopolies were necessary to stimulate the accumulation of capital and its investment in new lines of commerce. But in this view there are several misconceptions. (1) The choice was not one between trading by chartered monopolies like the Merchant Adventurers and *individual* enterprise, but between the grant of exclusive privileges to narrow cliques of merchants and a system of trade regulation which would have left room for the natural development of joint-stock enterprise. The latter principle was clearly recognized at an early period in English history. In the seventeenth century indeed it was usual for merchants engaged in foreign trade to join in partnership with others similarly employed in England or in foreign countries. They required no special privileges to press home upon them the advantages of such an arrangement for certain lines of commerce. Partnership was discussed as a well-recognized and generally accepted principle. (2) The trading companies were not chartered with the object of beginning and fostering new branches of foreign trade. The companies grew out of the associations which were formed for prosecuting discoveries. Free enterprise preceded the chartered company. A number of the more enterprising merchants would subscribe sums varying in magnitude for undertaking experimental voyages. Sometimes the major part of the expense was borne by a single merchant. When these more adventurous merchants had proved the possibility of opening up a profitable trade, they or a section of them secured the grant of a monopoly. This monopoly not infrequently excluded others who had as strong a claim as themselves. In the noteworthy case of the East India Company, it was several years after the grant of their charter before the majority of the members could be persuaded to risk their capital. (3) It was a matter of common notoriety at the beginning of the seventeenth century that if private traders cared to run the risk of infringing the charters of the companies, they could make large profits. (4) It seems probable that the development of foreign trade was in the main due to the successful efforts of the private traders. Towards the end of the seventeenth century they were irritated and hindered by the companies, but their very complaints prove that they were then able to laugh at the exclusive pretensions of these associations. When half a dozen merchants of Exeter could complain that their exports were five times those of the Merchant Adventurers, the company must have ceased to be a practical grievance. (5) The only really successful company was the East India Company. But its expansion did not arrive until it was put upon a national basis, and until the development of trade and commerce in other directions had given rise to a moneyed class who were willing to invest their savings in what promised great gains.

Hostility to the trading companies is a most marked feature of seventeenth-century history. But their opponents were isolated. Any one of them would have preferred a monopoly for himself. They were not strong enough for a long time to defy the companies' charters. Such a course involved, in addition to the risks of trade, which they would have been willing to undertake, the risk, nay the certainty of prolonged and expensive law-suits with powerful corporations, in which they would probably have been beaten. If on the formation of a "ring" in modern times outsiders were liable to heavy penalties, including the confiscation of their capital, and the law courts were certain to decide against them, it is evident that it would be a long time before competition asserted itself. Eventually the private traders became too numerous and too wealthy for the companies to fight them.

Until the end of the sixteenth century the Merchant Adventurers were the principal trading company, and they practically monopolized the foreign trade of the country. Their avowed object was to restrict supply and keep up prices. No one was allowed to export more than an amount fixed by the Company. The enhanced price would of course be paid by the foreign consumer, but such a policy must have reduced the demand for English woollen goods, small as it was at that time, below what it would have been in a normal condition of trade. The English manufacturers, on the other hand, felt the oppressive hand of the Merchant Adventurers in another way. If the complaints of the enemies of the Company have any weight, the manufacturers frequently had their goods left on their hands, or the Company would only purchase them at a price which scarcely allowed a reasonable profit. It is easy enough to see what would happen. The manufacturer would use every means to cheapen production, and to encourage an illicit trade. There were two ways in which economy was possible. (1) By adulteration, or the infringement of the cloth statutes; and (2) by cutting down wages. The Merchant Adventurers were constantly complaining of the deceits in the manufacture of cloth, and the attempts of the clothiers to turn the Statute of Apprenticeship to their own advantage are equally evident. It also seems clear that an illicit trade sprang up.

There are many striking differences between economic investigation in the seventeenth century and at the present time. The early writers were generally busy practical men, in whose lives there was neither time nor opportunity for diligent research. Some of them, it is to be feared, were in the position of Roger Coke, of whom it was said that "though, in his day, he had good speculative notions in trade, he was not so successful in the practice of it." Men wrote pamphlets, not because after a careful and impartial investigation they had discovered important principles which it was desirable that the world should know, but to defend the interests of some section whose interests were attacked, to support a project to which subscriptions were invited, or to urge some remedy for evils in the state. There was for the most part nothing wrong in this. We are in our own day inundated with publications of the same kind, but we do not rank them with scientific treatises. We must not expect an impartial view of the Merchant Adventurers from Wheeler, its paid secretary and advocate, or of the East India Company from Sir Josiah Child, first director and then chairman of the Company.

Another drawback which the writers felt keenly was the absence of reliable information on economic subjects. Sir William Petty, John Graunt, Gregory King, Davenant, and others made some interesting and useful calculations towards the end of the seventeenth century; but so late as 1699, Charles Davenant, who, as Commissioner of Excise, might be supposed to have exceptional opportunities for obtaining information of a certain kind, complains that "the aids and lights which might be gathered from the publick accompts and offices, have been industriously withheld from all who are not servile applauders of the wild and destructive conduct . . . . of some persons of no small power in the management of affairs." He speaks of Gregory King and himself as "beginners of an art not yet polish'd, and which time may bring to more perfection." "If our manner of inquiring be found instructive, we hope hereafter to be followed by abler hands who shall finish what we are but beginning."

The writers of this period used the ordinary language of business when they discussed economic questions. They wrote as merchants, and addressed themselves to that class even when they did not belong to it. We must therefore not expect scientific precision in the use of terms. Many of them, in their efforts to make themselves clear, used "a multitude of words which, in discourses of this nature especially, doth more puzzle the cause than give a clear understanding of the matter." Many of the phrases which we find in the pamphlets of the seventeenth century are still in common use. But no one when he hears men talk of a "favourable" or "unfavourable state of the exchanges," supposes that their heads are full of economic fallacies. He knows that such expressions are used to convey certain information about the state of the money market, not to enunciate a theory of international exchange. If, however, the business man based an economic system on assumptions derived from a misinterpretation of these loose phrases, it is easy to imagine what would follow. This was precisely what happened in the seventeenth century. So far as the erroneous principles of the Mercantile System became the basis of a well-defined policy, the results were disastrous. But it is only true in a very general sense that the Mercantile System was "the theoretical counterpart of the practical activities of the age." Their practical activities were more important and more true than their theories. It would be as fair to judge the working-classes from their speeches at labour meetings as to judge the seventeenth century from its economic pamphlets. Finally, it must be said that the questions which these men discussed were extremely difficult and complex—questions on which there is great diversity of opinion amongst the most skilled economists of our own day.

Keeping these considerations in mind, let us examine some of the controversies of the seventeenth century. Not the least of the difficulties which followed the debasement of the currency was the shrinkage of the royal revenues. Elizabeth tried to remedy the evil by decrying the coinage, but this expedient was unsuccessful. It is not improbable that the Government was actually defrauded of large sums, for the destruction of the old Staple System and the inefficiency of the Customs organization was favourable to such a result. Two courses naturally suggested themselves. The reactionary party longed for the revival of the old system; the progressives looked to improvements in organization to meet the changed conditions of trade and commerce. The latter policy was adopted, and aroused the strongest objections. Nor is it possible to conclude that there was no ground for the complaints which found expression in the writings of Thomas Milles, for some time Commissioner of the Customs at Sandwich. The Supervisors, who were appointed to screw the revenue to a higher pitch, probably made a good thing of it for themselves without any proportionate advantage to the Crown; while the Custumers, as they were called, were irritated by the new officials. Nor did their discontent rest there. The merchants had their grievances, and "repined thereat." They resented the arbitrary impositions to which they were subjected, "appealinge to the positive lawes of Trafique as theire *generall inheritance*, and the Strangers urging onely theire treaties and mutuall contracts." Thomas Milles laid down the general principle, which should underlie all taxes on commodities, that "the form and manner of collection should be fit and answerable to the matter and persons," and that there should be "certainty" and "indifference of assessment." They claimed that these canons of taxation, if we may use an expression of a later day, were not fulfilled. "Whereas, in the payments on landes and goods, the collector alone being satisfied, the partie is acquit, without further charge, trouble, or delay: in the matter of merchandize, beside the Prince's and Collectors' due, Impositions and a multiplicitie of irregular exactions and fees to Searchers, Comptrollers, etc., is such a secrete burden, that in 5 or 6 years the payments in this kinde doe countervaile theire stockes. Privatly they grieve that amongst themselves Trades under Companies and societies are drawne and abridged into a few men's hands; wherein, besides the wrong offered to the law and generall freedome of the land, even within themselves also, the wealthier and best grounded, by oddes of stockes, restraints, and other advantages, drive the weaker to the walls. That one Porte (London) seems to give Law to all the rest, without warrant of Law, reason or Pollicie; the daunger whereof, moe see and lament then know how to prevent or remedie. That in all Ports extremities attend them, driving them to this issue, either to quit their Trades altogether, or to worke it out by favour at one porte or other, to the displeasure of the Prince." The latter course was probably more usually followed; and if Milles, a man entrusted by the Government with some not unimportant affairs, is to be believed, the Supervisors connived at frauds on the revenue, and took fees for so doing. The Custumers also had their grievances, which presumably would make them less zealous in the discharge of their duties. Milles supposes each one to have the charge of five out-ports. He then reckons up the charges to which they were subjected as follows:—(1) They were liable to the expenses and hazards incident to custom causes. (2) There were no custom-houses in the out-ports, no public wharves, cranes, nor store-houses, "to the Prince's daily loss and the Custumer's disadvantage." The Custumer himself had to provide, hire, and furnish a custom-house, the yearly rent alone of which would not amount to less than 40*s*. (3) Then at each custom-house "must be entertained a discreet person," who could not be offered less than twenty marks wages, and as much for diet. The charge under this head for five out-ports was put down at £200 per annum. (4) Ink, paper, parchment, etc., involved an additional charge of £10 per annum. "Besides, the hazard of the Queen's money that of necessitie is to passe by Bils of Exchange through sundry hands (being allowed no passage-money) is an unknowne hazard, trouble, and care to the Custumers onely, which the rest (*i. e.* the supervisors) breake no sleepe for." Milles condemned the system of farming the customs, and argued that the way to increase the returns from this source was "by traffic and free commerce." We have not space to describe in detail the measures by which the customs and revenue were put upon a sound basis. Observations of this nature might be given in scores. Enough perhaps has been said to explain the great importance, throughout the seventeenth century, which was attached to the development of trade and commerce as a source of revenue. It is no matter of surprise that, dissatisfied with the system in vogue and alarmed at the condition of the revenue, some writers at the beginning of the seventeenth century looked for relief to the revival of the stringent regulations of the Staple System, and associated with it a degree of efficiency which it never possessed. The labours of Walpole, Pitt, Huskisson, and others, taken in conjunction with the vast growth of wealth, have removed far from us the fears of the seventeenth century. We "breake no sleepe" about the revenue, however unrestful the Chancellor of the Exchequer may be, but we can understand why the subject assumed such prominence in the minds of the mercantilists, and how it came about that even Adam Smith said that one of the two principal objects of Political Economy was "to supply the state or commonwealth with a revenue sufficient for the public services." We can leave the matter to the Chancellor of the Exchequer, and grumble till we obtain "indifference of assessment."

From questions of this nature we pass naturally to the foreign exchanges. Here we find ourselves inundated with pamphlet literature, correspondence, and state papers. The Greshams, Sir Robert Cotton, Sir Walter Raleigh, Sir William Beecher, Sir Francis Knowles, Andrew Palmer, Gerard Malynes, and Edward Misselden are some amongst the many men who devoted attention to the subject and endeavoured to find out correct principles of foreign exchange. It must not be forgotten that when they complained of the frequent exportation of bullion they had no imaginary inconvenience in their minds, but that there was a real "scarcity of money" for the ordinary purposes of trade, which was acutely felt during the recoinage of Elizabeth. Letters from various parts of the country are conclusive on this point. The events were fresh in the minds of all at the beginning of the seventeenth century; indeed, the recoinage had only mitigated, it had not removed difficulties which continued to be felt until the great recoinage in 1696. From the names mentioned above we may select those of Malynes and Misselden, for they well represent the two aspects of the controversy about the exchanges. Malynes is not the least interesting amongst the remarkable men of this epoch. He was one of the first English writers in whose works we find that conception of Natural Law which was later on to play such an important part in the development of economic science. He doubtless borrowed it from Roman Law, in which he appears to have been well read. "This law of merchants, or *Lex Mercatoria*," he says in one place, "in the fundamentals of it, is nothing else but (as Cicero defineth true and just law) *Recta Ratio, naturae congruens, diffusa in omnes, constans sempiterna.* . . . Even as the bills, contracts, or Testaments of particular men, cannot derogate or undoe the Ordinances of the magistrates, and as the order of the magistrates cannot abolish ancient good customes, nor customes cannot abridge the generall Lawes of an absolute Prince; no more can the Law of Princes alter or change the Law of God and Nature." Malynes' philosophy, however, is for the most part a mere jumble of old-world metaphysics. He was deeply versed in the lore of the alchemists, had read "all the books of Paracelsus," followed with interest Ripley's *Twelve Operations*, and expected the discovery of a *Prima Materia.* But Malynes was not merely philosopher and alchemist. We find him turning over the Tower records for information about trade and commerce under Edward III., and reading with interest a scarce manuscript at Lambeth. His great folio

Lex Mercatoria (1622) bears witness to his "fiftie yeares observation, knowledge, and experience." He was not sparing in invective when his anger was roused, and he denounced his opponents in vigorous language when they touched on his favourite topic, the foreign exchanges. But on most subjects he was fair, temperate, and judicial. He hated extremes, and spoke scornfully of what he considered the false scruples and the hair-splitting of "those precise men, by some called Puritans." "To these weake stomacks thus troubled with a nausea, I would not minister any cordials, electuaries or potions, to rid them of that distemperate humor; but a plaine vomit is fittest, the moone being in Aries or Capricorne." Malynes' practical experience as a merchant was great, and brought him into contact with men of all kinds. His books abound with little touches which show that he was familiar with, and had been engaged in, business transactions at most of the great cities of European commerce. We find him buying from Sir Francis Drake the pearls which he brought back after his successful raid on Carthagena in 1587, discussing mining with Sir Walter Raleigh, and experimenting on the properties of diamonds. He had a wide knowledge of Mint affairs, for he was one of the Assay Masters, sat on the Royal Commission of 1609, and was associated with the not very creditable scheme for a coinage of brass farthings. But he did not gain by his share in the transaction, for we find him shortly afterwards in the Fleet Prison. His petition to the king (February 16th, 1619) for relief is very quaint. He complains that he had been ruined by his employers, who insisted on paying him in his own farthings, "which were rendered void by a subsequent unauthorized coinage thereof." Malynes indeed seems not to have been very successful in business. In his dedicatory letter to Sir Robert Cecil, prefixed to the *Canker of England's Commonwealth* (March 18th, 1601), he says, "If it shall be objected, that my case seemeth to extend to the welfare and upholding of a commonwealth, which is nothing else but a great household, and that I can hardly maintain my own little cottage or family, I will confess my own infirmity." But he points out that his difficulties were caused by "encounters and injuries." Twenty years later Misselden rather meanly scoffs at his arguments, which were "as threadbare as his coat."

Misselden is not such an interesting person as his antagonist. He was a member of the Merchant Adventurers' Company, and for some time acted as deputy-governor at Delft. It appears that their cloth trade was falling off, and we find Misselden investigating the causes of its decay in 1620. In a letter from Hackney (April 17th, 1620), he attributes it to abuses in searching and sealing, "persons being employed who are negligent and ignorant, and the seals publicly sold, so that clothiers affix them to goods never seen by the searcher, which causes great diminution in the demand for and price of English cloths abroad." He suggests a more rigorous mode of search. There is no reason for thinking that the woollen trade was decaying at this time. The evidence points to the opposite conclusion. That the Merchant Adventurers found the demand for their goods diminishing, and prices falling, points to the success of the outsiders, who could undersell them. Misselden acted as one of the commissioners on behalf of the East India Company in the treaty negotiations at Amsterdam in 1622 and 1623. He was patronized by Laud, and published a *Book of Ecclesiastical Policy*, in addition to his economical works. He seconded the attempts of Sir William Boswell, the English minister at the Hague, to carry out Laud's instructions and thrust the Prayer-Book on the English residents at Delft (March 1633).

These remarks will make clear the relative position of the two disputants. Malynes was perfectly aware that certain elements, such as time, distance, and the state of credit, entered into the determination of the value of bills of exchange. This was one of the elementary truths which merchants learnt as soon as they adopted this method of avoiding the transmission of bullion. It was indeed stated in the grant to Sir Thomas Boleyn (1509) of the custody of the exchanges at London and Calais. In these early times, it is possible that the king's officials could maintain a certain ratio of exchange for some time after it had ceased to represent the mutual indebtedness of England and foreign countries; that, in fact, there was an appearance of truth in Malynes' expression, "Exchange dominates commodities." When the functions of the King's Exchanger passed to the cambists and goldsmiths, the profits on discounting bills, which had formerly gone to the Royal Exchequer, went into their pockets. In the eyes of many people this simply meant that a number of irresponsible persons were defrauding the revenue and amassing wealth at the expense of the king. It may also be pointed out that the terms of exchange were determined in the days of Malynes, not by free competition, but by mutual agreement amongst the exchangers, who met together and fixed the rate after consulting on the state of the market. Practically, taking an average over a number of years, the result would not differ widely from that which would be reached by free competition. But it must be admitted that the mode in which these transactions were carried out gave many opportunities to the exchangers to anticipate or postpone the operation of natural causes. Difficulty of communication, ignorance of the real state of the market, and the friction of international trade caused the rate of the foreign exchanges to differ more widely from what we may call the normal rate than is possible at the present time.

If these considerations are borne in mind, and we remember the strong feeling which existed against all forms of usurious exaction, it is easy to understand Malynes' view of the "predominance of exchange," his denunciation of the "tricks of the exchangers," and his earnest appeal that exchanges should be settled, subject to those elements of time, distance, and the credit of the merchants on the principle of *Par pro Pari, value for value.* The fluctuations of the rate of exchange represented to his mind nothing which was the outcome of economic causes, but departures from the rule of upright conduct. He translated *Par pro Pari* into "*Do as you would be done by.*" When the state of the exchanges was against England, he thought, as many others thought, that the exchangers were deliberately undervaluing the king's coins to fill their own pockets. So we have his vigorous pamphlets, *The Canker of England's Commonwealth* (March 1601) and *St. George for England* (May 1601). He thought the old system should be revived. It has been suggested that he recommended this course from interested motives, he himself hoping to obtain a lucrative office under the King's Exchanger. If this was so, he must have had a singularly hopeful temperament, for he advocated the same views for more than forty years, long after there was any chance of their realization. In *St. George for England*, the dragon was *Foenus politicum*, his two wings *Usura palliata* and *usura explicata*, while his tail was the inconstant *Cambium*. The virgin was the King's Treasure and St. George the Royal Authority. Cut off the dragon's tail, said Malynes—*i. e.*, put down the exchangers—and all would be well with the trade and commerce of the country. The Government was really uncertain what course it would be best to pursue. Lord Burleigh held a patent as King's Exchanger for many years, without using it, and attempts were made to revive the old system. But in 1608 the Goldsmiths presented a petition against the appointment of an Exchanger, and the moneyed men of the city were too useful to be slighted. They contended that the revival of the office would be hurtful. It was "only used in the tyme of ignorance, when goldsmiths were fewe and pore, not able to buy bullion. . . . Yt will take away the freedome of everie subject to bring Bullion to the Mynt to be coyned." It would hinder importation and further exportation of gold and silver, and in addition to the "overthrowe of the whole trade and misterie of goldsmithes," it would raise the price of plate, reduce subsidies and tenths £300 per annum, prejudice the trade of the Mint, and benefit only the Exchanger.

The pamphlets of the years 1621—1623 appear to have been intended to deal with the subjects of inquiry by the Standing Commission on Trade, which was appointed on October 21st, 1622. There had previously been a committee of twelve persons to investigate the causes of the alleged decay of trade. These had reported from time to time, and attempts had been made to remedy by proclamation the evils which they pointed out. It was felt, however, that the "case was important and required constant regulation," so it was decided to appoint a Standing Commission to report from time to time and suggest remedies. The East India Company was strongly represented, for amongst the Commissioners were Sir Dudley Digges, Sir John Wolstenholme, Henry Garraway, Anthony Abdy, and Thomas Mun. The last-mentioned was afterwards Deputy-Governor of the Company. The instructions of the Commission were of a comprehensive character, for they were to inquire into the following points: The causes of the fall in the price of wool and woollen yarn, and the means of restoring it; the best means of preventing the exportation of wool and woollen yarn, fuller's-earth, and wood ashes, and of securing the importation of Irish and Scotch wool not manufactured at home; how to provide against a glut of woollens; improvements and prevention of deceits in the manufacture; whether the ordinances of the Merchant Adventurers, and other societies of merchants and handicraftsmen, unduly raised the price of woollen cloth; how far the trading companies acted as a restraint on trade; the advisability of meeting the wishes of outsiders by making trade more free and open; the best means of achieving this object, with a due regard to the necessary regulation of trade; how far joint-stock companies were beneficial or otherwise; how to remedy the unusual scarcity of money; the means of securing the importation of coin and bullion; whether the balance of trade was unfavourable to England through an excess of imports over exports; and, "above other things, seriously and carefully to consider by what good means the navy and shipping of the kingdom might be best maintained and enlarged, and mariners bred up and increased." With a view to advancing these objects, the Commissioners were instructed to consider, amongst other means, the following:—The development of the herring fishery "by our people for the common good"; the administration of the navigation laws then in force "to the end that the shipping of other nations may not be employed for importing foreign commodities whilst our own shipping want employment"; the advisability of enforcing the Statutes of Employment; and finally, "because the East India Company have been much taxed by many for exporting the coin and treasure of this realm, to furnish their trade withal, or that which would otherwise have come in hither, for the use of our subjects, and that they do not return such merchandize from India as doth recompense that loss unto our kingdom; we authorize you to inquire and search whether that company do truly and justly perform their contract with us concerning the exportation of money, and by what means that trade, which is specious in show, may be made profitable to the kingdom."

The instructions to the Commission of 1622 are a good summary of the economic questions which engaged the attention of merchants during the first half of the seventeenth century. Thomas Mun had already replied to some of them in the defence of the East India Company, which he published in 1621. In that work, *Discourse of Trade from England to the East Indies*, he pointed out the advantages of the East India Company to the kingdom in the lower prices for the products of the East, rebutted the charges brought against the Company, and indicated in what manner the exportation of bullion was beneficial. He approved, however, of the Statutes of Employment, an opinion which he afterwards changed. We have seen Misselden writing about the causes of the decay of the cloth trade. In 1622 he published his *Free Trade, or the Means to make Trade Flourish*. This pamphlet expressed his views on the subjects which engaged the attention of the Commission. It is on the same lines as the letter which has already been quoted. Thirty years later, indeed, he still held the opinion that the principal reason for the backwardness of the English cloth trade was the adulteration which was practised by the manufacturers. But Misselden was a firm believer in the necessity of the Company organization; the prevailing discontent and the instructions to the Commission made it desirable to put forward the strongest possible arguments in their behalf. He pointed to the successful commerce which was carried on where these companies existed, and compared the results they achieved with those of the "open trades." He was evidently anxious to conciliate as far as possible those who were opposed to the Companies. He therefore tried to disarm the opposition to the regulated companies and turn it against the joint-stock associations, by his absurd definition of "monopoly" (*vide* p. 9). He especially objected to the East India Company, and their exportation of bullion. This seems strange and disingenuous unless he changed his mind before he wrote his next work, for he then expressed quite opposite views. In 1622 also he was in the employment of the East India Company. There was much in Misselden's book with which Malynes probably agreed; but to see the decay of trade and the scarcity of money attributed to such causes as the excessive consumption of foreign commodities, the exportation of bullion by the East India Company, and defective searching in the cloth trade, was more than he could endure, after his life-long hewing at the dragon's tail. So he rushed into the fray with a pamphlet entitled the *Maintenance of Free Trade*, the "little fish" which was to precede his "great whale," *Lex Mercatoria*, published shortly afterwards. He complained bitterly that Misselden had omitted "to handle the predominant part of trade, namely, the mystery of Exchange." "This rule is infallible: that when the Exchange doth answer the true value of our moneys according to their intrinsicke weight and fineness, and their extrinsicke valuation, they are never exported, because the gayne is answered by exchange, which is the cause of transportation. This cause being prevented maketh the effect to cease." He enumerated many "admirable feats to bee done by exchange," which "overruled the price of moneys and commodities." He defended the East India Company on the ground that "it was convenient to have joint stocks for distant places," and spoke with approval of Mun's *Discourse* on the East India trade. It was "overballancing" that caused the exportation of bullion. He exposed the absurdity of Misselden's definition of monopoly, and attacked the regulated companies, especially the Merchant Adventurers, pointing to their opposition to the development of the fisheries.

Misselden replied in the *Circle of Commerce, or the Ballance of Trade*, etc. (1623), a large portion of which was devoted to a refutation of Malynes' theory of exchange. But he lost his temper in dealing with his opponent. "Malynes himself," he said, "his subject, much more his rude stile and unmannerly manner of writing, deserve contempt rather than the honour of an answer." He accused Malynes of stealing from Thomas Milles' *Custumer's Reply*, and demolished his theory of exchange. "It is not the rate of exchange, whether it be higher or lower, that maketh the price of commodities deare or cheape, as Malynes would inferre; but it is the plenty or scarcitie of commodities, their use or non-use, that maketh them rise and fall in price. Otherwise, if Malynes' rule were true that the prices of commodities should perpetually follow the rates of exchange, then commodities should all rise and fall together, as the exchange riseth or falleth." . . . "But . . . . commonly one commodity riseth when another falleth; and they fall and rise as they are more or lesse in request and use." Misselden denied the charges against the Companies. "But," he said, "there's no discourse of Free Trade will please Malynes, and others of his minde, without a Par of exchange, or complaint against companies, the Merchant Adventurers especially." The rest of Misselden's book was devoted to an examination of the balance of trade. He made some interesting calculations about the relative amount of imports and exports in 1608 and 1622, and concluded that while in the former year the balance was favourable to this country, it had since become unfavourable. The theory which he stated differs in no important respect from that which appeared afterwards in Mun's *England's Treasure by Foreign Trade*, except that the former is less elaborated, and less systematic than the latter. The question whether Mun was indebted to Misselden, or Misselden to Mun, is of no importance. They were contemporaries, and must have known each other, for Mun was deputy-governor of the East India Company while Misselden was acting on their behalf in the Amboyna negotiations. Neither writer had any originality, but they could express with sufficient clearness the views generally current amongst the members of the trading companies, and that was the secret of their influence. The theory of the balance of trade formed in the hands of Thomas Mun a powerful defence of the East India Company. After Misselden's book, the next step in the development of the theory was the Petition and Remonstrance of the East India Company (1628). This was written by Thomas Mun, and presented to the House of Commons in October 1628. It was found to be so useful an apology for the exportation of bullion that it was reprinted in 1641. In the sphere of practical statesmanship the balance of trade was appealed to as a test of economic prosperity. We have already seen an instance of this in the instructions to the Commission of 1622. Strafford, commenting on the trade of Ireland (July 25th, 1636), regards the excess of exports over imports as "a certain sign that that Commonwealth gains upon their neighbours;" and Cromwell's Act for the exportation of native commodities states "that the prosperous estate of all islands is very much (under God) maintained and supported by a quick and flourishing trade, and in a just endeavour and care, that the exportation of the native commodities overbalances the importation of foreign commodities."

Mun incorporated the arguments of the Petition and Remonstrance in his well-known book, *England's Treasure by Foreign Trade*. This work, which was probably written between 1641 and 1651, was not published until 1664, some years after the death of the author. Its origin in the defence of the East India Company against the charges of its enemies should be kept in mind. It was not intended as an exhaustive and systematic treatise on the economic questions of the seventeenth century. Mun proposed to discuss so much of the merchant's practice "as concerned the bringing of Treasure into the kingdom." Drawing an analogy between a state and an individual with a certain revenue and ready-money, he stated at the outset the practical rule which must be constantly observed in international trade. This rule, the basis of Mun's system, was "to sell more to strangers yearly than wee consume of theirs in value." He then discussed the following methods of increasing exportation and of diminishing the consumption of foreign wares. (1) Waste lands, etc. should be cultivated, to prevent the importation of foreign-grown hemp, flax, cordage, and tobacco. (2) People should refrain from luxuries,—"vices at this present more notorious than in former ages." Mun approved of sumptuary laws and laws enjoining the consumption of home manufactures, rather than prohibitions of foreign goods. This recommendation must be taken in conjunction with another which rested on a distinction he made between natural and artificial wealth. The natural wealth of the community must be expended as frugally as possible, so that the surplus for exportation might be greater. If the people, however, would have luxuries, let them be home manufactures, "where the excess of the rich might be the employment of the poor." The latter, however, would be more profitably employed in the manufacture of goods for foreign markets. (3) The manufacture of goods which could not be produced abroad should be encouraged, and we should "endeavour to sell them dear, so far forth as the high price cause not a less vent in the quantity." Commodities for which foreign nations could have recourse to other markets must be sold as cheaply as possible. Mun estimated that a fall in price of 25 per cent. meant an increase of 50 per cent. in the "bulk of trade, for the benefit of the public." (4) Generally speaking, "commerce should be free to strangers to bring in and carry out at their pleasure," but we should endeavour to "use our own shipping and so get the merchant's gains, insurance, and freight." This was the economic principle on which the Navigation Act was defended. We have already seen that the Trade Commissioners in 1622 were directed to inquire into the administration of the then existing Navigation Laws with a view to the employment of our own shipping. English merchants saw the great gains of Holland through their monopoly of the carrying trade of the world, and they desired to share in it. (5) The fishing trade, "our natural wealth," should be developed. Apart from all political considerations of the importance of the fishing-trade as a "nursery for mariners," the economic writers of the seventeenth century urged its development on quite distinct economical grounds. At a time when English manufactures were few, and with the example of Holland to stimulate activity, it can only be a matter for surprise that England did not more persistently develop such an obvious source of prosperity as the fisheries. The Dutch regarded their fishing, which was carried on mainly in English waters, as their "chiefest trade," and the foundation of their prosperity. (6) England should be made a staple for foreign goods to be re-exported, and should "esteem and cherish those trades which we have in remote and far countreys," such as the trade to the East Indies. In this way we should obtain foreign goods on cheaper terms and gain by re-exportation. (7) It was beneficial to export money as well as wares. To make this position clear, Mun devoted a separate chapter to a recapitulation of the arguments he had stated in the Petition and Remonstrance of 1622. By the exportation of bullion, wares could be purchased which could afterwards be re-exported to foreign countries, and being there sold for a large profit, might bring back more treasure than was originally sent out to purchase them. He drew an analogy from the seed-time and harvest of agriculture. "If we only behold the actions of the husbandman in the seed-time, when he casteth away much good corn into the ground, we shall account him rather a madman than a husbandman. But when we consider his labours in the harvest, which is the end of his endeavours, we shall find the worth and plentiful increase of his actions." (8) Manufactures made of foreign materials should be exported custom free. This would increase "the value of our stock yearly issued into other countreys," and "would cause more foreign materials to be brought in, to the improvement of his Majesty's customs." (9) Export duties should be low, "lest by endearing native commodities to the stranger it hinder their

ENGLISH TRADE AND FINANCE.

CHAPTER I.

THE MONOPOLIES.

THERE are few subjects of greater importance to the student of economics than the history of inventions, for in it he has the key to the most far-reaching changes in industry and commerce. It is fitting, therefore, to commence this brief review of some seventeenth century changes with an account of the monopolies or patents, which aroused perhaps the first great outbreak of popular indignation against unwise restrictions on internal trade. This will bring the economic activities of the seventeenth century into relation with more recent movements.

We have already seen the origin of the practice of granting monopolies for new inventions, or for the introduction of a new process from abroad. Confined within these limits, few people would have complained of so reasonable a practice. But, in the unsettled state of opinion in the sixteenth century on trade subjects, it was not easy to discriminate between the forms of industrial activity which did or did not require protection for their further development; and the practice of granting monopolies soon extended even to the sale of articles of general consumption. It was this abuse which aroused popular indignation. Before, however, we pass judgment on Queen Elizabeth and her counsellors, we must put ourselves in their position, and try to understand their motives and the difficulties they had to surmount. There have never been wanting unscrupulous or ignorant people too ready to take advantage of a prevailing prejudice, or too easily inclined to believe the interests of the community coincident with their own. It is not only in past ages that large classes have been glad to cloke their selfish designs in the garb of economic orthodoxy.

There were several causes likely to make the monopolies a grave abuse. It was not well understood within what limits they might be legally granted. Laurence Hide, who led the attack in the House of Commons in 1601, quoted a precedent of 50 Edward III., when a certain John Peach was fined and imprisoned for obtaining a monopoly of the sale of sweet wines. In the time of James I. it was recognized that a monopoly might be granted for a new invention, or for the introduction of a new process from abroad, but that any further extension of the principle was illegal. Granting this, however, there was room for much discussion as to what might be included within these limits, and many cases, which involved important considerations of State policy, might fall outside such a definition. In the seventeenth century, for example, it might be argued from the mercantilist point of view that it was unwise to leave the manufacture of gold and silver thread to private enterprise. The manufacture of gunpowder, saltpetre, and iron ordnance might with equal justice be considered fit subjects for monopolies under Government control. Patent law, as we understand it now, was virtually non-existent.

Again, the limits of the Royal prerogative in the regulation of trade, so far from being defined, were not even debated. When the Commons petitioned against the monopolies in 1597, the Queen "hoped that her dutiful and loving subjects would not take away her prerogative, which was the chiefest flower in her garden, and the principal and head pearl in her crown and diadem; but that they would leave that to her disposition." King James expressed himself with greater emphasis on more than one occasion. The Monopoly Bill of 1621 was rejected by the Lords mainly on the ground that it encroached on the Royal prerogative. Bacon held that the Queen, by virtue of her prerogative, might set at liberty things restrained by Statute Law or otherwise; restrain things that are at liberty—for example, grant a monopoly for a new invention, or when there was "a glut of things"; and grant a license of transportation to one man, when there was a scarcity. "I say, and I say again, that we ought not to meddle with, or judge, of her Majesty's prerogative." Such a definition of the limits of the Queen's authority in the regulation of trade might be easily stretched to cover all the monopolies to which objection was made.

The idea of diverting a share in the gains of commerce into the Royal Exchequer was at the root of some of the characteristic principles of the mercantile system. In accordance with this idea a yearly payment to the King, the amount of which varied with the expected profits of the undertaking, was usually stipulated for in the patent grants for new inventions. Returns from this source, however, were too meagre to furnish the only motive for granting monopolies. In the time of James I., Mr. Gardiner says, they did not amount to £900 per annum. It is not unlikely that the Exchequer was the poorer when the King himself became the patentee, and took the risk of the undertaking. For example, conditional letters patent were granted in 1604 to Lord Sheffield and others for the sole making of alum in Yorkshire. It is said that they lost £33,000, and "could not proceed any further without bringing in new men." They then obtained a patent for all Great Britain and Ireland, but succeeded no better; for they lost £40,000, and "no allomes made to benefit, although the price was raised at a certaintie and all foreign allomes prohibited to come in." Other examples would show that the revenue derived from this source in the seventeenth century could not have been large, and even when profits were considerable, it would be easy to elude the vigilance of the Government. But, if the direct advantages of the monopolies to the Government as a source of revenue were meagre, they offered a convenient method of strengthening the loyalty or of rewarding the services of courtiers. It is difficult on any other hypothesis to explain the numerous grants of Elizabeth, many of which were made to persons who had no possible connection with trade, but valued the monopoly merely as a source of gain. Even Bacon appears to have considered such grants an injustice. In a letter to the Earl of Essex, who had a monopoly of the sale of sweet wines, he advised him to have nothing to do with "monopolies or any oppressions." It was the sense of injustice, the inconvenience entailed by the monopolies, and the belief that they were granted for the gain of individuals, and not for the benefit of the people, that aroused popular indignation. This first found expression in the Parliament of 1597, when a motion was introduced "touching sundry enormities growing by patents of privilege and monopolies." The Commons apparently did not then realize that this was an attack on the royal prerogative, for they discussed the question quite freely for several days. The struggle came in the last Parliament of Elizabeth (1601), and the report of the debates, preserved in Townshend's *Historical Memorials*, gives the best account of contemporary opinion. Townshend was himself a member of the House, and took a prominent part in directing the right course to be pursued.

Mr. Dyott, of the Middle Temple, began the attack by moving for an Act against patents. "There be many commodities in this realm which, being public for the benefit of every particular subject, are monopolized by patent from her Majesty, only for the good and private gain of one man." He was followed by Mr. Laurence Hide, who moved for an exposition "of the common law, touching these kind of patents, commonly called monopolies." The list of those complained of included salt, steel, tin, starch, stone bottles, glass pots, etc. It was urged that the effect of the monopolies had been greatly to enhance prices. For example, it was said that steel had risen in price from £12 10*s*. to £19 the barrel, or from 2½*d*. to 5*d*. a pound; and that the monopoly "had been the utter undoing of all edge-tool makers." Starch was said to have increased from 18*s*. to 50*s*. and 56*s*.; the price of stone bottles had doubled since the patent; glasses had risen from 1*s*. 4*d*. to 5*s*. and 3*s*. 4*d*. to 9*s*. a dozen. But no trust can be put in these figures. The numerous complaints and prosecutions for the infringement of monopolies in the reign of James I. show that it was practically impossible to exclude competition, and general prices were probably not much affected. The Commons also complained that the monopolies brought "the general profit into a private hand;" "that the inward and private commodities of the kingdom dare not be used without license of the monopolists;" and that the existence of such abuses encouraged a spirit of disloyalty to the Queen. "There is no Act of her Majesty that hath been or is more derogatory to her own Majesty, or more odious to the subject, or more dangerous to the Commonwealth, than the granting of these monopolies." They gave the instances of aqua vitæ and vinegar, in which the substitutes of the patentees had forced sellers to compound with them, and they complained that while some were void in their effects, all monopolies were hateful in principle. Bacon and Cecil, on the other hand, defended this exercise of the Royal prerogative, and counselled great caution in approaching the Queen on the matter. Sir Walter Raleigh, "in a sharp speech," maintained that the tin-miners had received higher and more certain wages since his monopoly than before. It was also explained that the petition of the Commons in 1597 would have received attention but for the want of time and the pressure of other business. There was much discussion as to whether the Commons should proceed by Bill or by petition. Townshend recommended the middle course of petitioning for leave to pass a Bill. The Queen, however, anticipated them by sending a message through the Speaker promising redress. She met the whole Commons at Whitehall on the 30th, and in a speech of great tact, extricated herself from a difficult position by yielding what was asked for. She thanked them for drawing attention to the evils, "for had I not received a knowledge from you, I might have fallen into the lapse of an error." To those who had used too plain language in the House she said, "I am not so simple to suppose but that there are some of the Lower House whom these grievances never touched. And for them, I think they spake out of zeal for their countries, and not out of spleen or malevolent affection, as being the parties grieved. And I take it exceeding gratefully from them; because it gives us to know, that no respects or interests had moved them other than the minds they have to suffer no diminution of our honour, and our subjects' loves unto us. That my grants should be grievous to my people, and oppressions privileged under colour of our patents, our kingly dignity shall not suffer it; yea, when I heard it, I could not give rest unto my thoughts until I had reformed it."

Elizabeth's promises were only partially fulfilled. She issued a proclamation, recalling some of the most obnoxious patents, and left the rest to the due course of the law. Various interests had gathered round them which it was inconvenient to disturb, and more pressing difficulties diverted attention from the abuses which had aroused the indignation of the Commons. Four days after his accession James issued a proclamation, restraining the monopolies until the Council were satisfied that they were attended with no evil results. He also spoke strongly against them in his first Parliament. He declared monopolies to be contrary to the laws, but was favourable to patents for new inventions, provided they were not illegal, mischievous to the State by raising the prices of commodities at home, or hurtful to trade.

But new monopolies were soon granted, and, in fact, the abuses appear to have been greater than they were in the time of Elizabeth. The loud complaints of his people obliged James in 1610 to revoke all the monopolies by proclamation, but, unable to keep his promises, he was immediately led into new ones. At last, after a prolonged agitation, the Commons obtained in 1624 the Statute of Monopolies. By this famous statute, which is still the basis of English patent law, to confer on any individual the exclusive right of carrying on a particular trade or manufacture, was in general declared to be beyond the limits of the prerogative and contrary to the common law. An exception, however, was made in favour of new inventions, for which a monopoly might be granted for fourteen years, on the ground that the practice encouraged ingenuity, and encroached on no right of which others were in possession. The Act also did not extend to certain municipal privileges, to trading companies, to the manufacture of gunpowder, which was the monopoly of the Crown, or to the monopolies of glass-making, smalt, and smelting iron. It is interesting to notice that the law of copyright has grown out of the Statute of Monopolies. The right of authors in this respect was not defined until quite late in our history. Books were included in the ordinary monopoly lists, and it was a vexed question during the seventeenth century whether they came within the meaning of the statute. An attempt was made to settle the matter early in the reign of Anne; the law of copyright, however, was not put on a sound basis until 1774. It was for a long time doubtful whether a copyright extended to an oral lecture. It was decided in the affirmative, if the lecturer sent notice of the lecture in writing to two justices of the peace living within five miles of the place of delivery two days before the lecture was given.

The Statute of Monopolies was a real gain, although it left untouched some of the most vexatious restrictions on trade. (1) Grants of special privileges to individuals like those complained of in the last Parliament of Elizabeth were declared illegal. (2) It left the way open for an attack upon the exclusive trading corporations; for, though they were excepted from the operation of the statute, it was open to discussion, when their charters expired, whether they could be renewed without parliamentary sanction. (3) When Charles, like his father, ignored the statute and continued to grant monopolies to increase his revenue, it placed him in an illegal position. The Lords justly included monopolies among grievances in the Remonstrance presented to the King at York in 1640, praying him to summon Parliament.

The agitation against the monopolies in the seventeenth century has left its mark on the pamphlet literature of the time, and helped in the formation of opinion on this subject. Edward Misselden distinguished between a monopoly or restraint of trade, and the ordering or government of trade by means of companies. In his view, a monopoly implied "the restraint of the liberty of commerce to some one or few, and the setting of the price at the pleasure of Monopolitan to his private benefit, and the prejudice of the public. . . . Unless these two parts concurre in a monopoly, it cannot truly and properly bee so-called, nor ought it so to be accounted." Such a monopoly he held to be contrary to equity and public utility, but he approved of "the pre-emption of time" granted to some persons by letters patent, and of patents for new inventions. Gerard Malynes divided monopolies into three classes:—(1) *reasonable:* "such things and trifles as are a pleasure, as starch, cards, lute strings, tobacco," etc.; (2) *unreasonable:* e.g. flesh, fish, butter, cheese, "or needfull things for the sustenance of man, without which he can hardly live civilly"; (3) *indifferent:* e.g. velvets, silks, sugar, spices, "and other delicacies and dainties or curiosities, indifferent to be used or not." He defined a monopoly as "a kind of commerce in buying, selling, changing, or bartering, usurped by a few, and sometimes but by one person, and forestalled from all others, to his or theire privat gaine, and to the hurt and detriment of other men; whereby of course, or by authoritie, the libertie of trade is restrained from others, whereby the monopolist is enabled to set a price of commodities at his pleasure." Malynes did not believe in the encouragement of trade by these means. He ridiculed the Company of Royal Mines established by James I. "There is none of that company that doth advance any works that I can learn." He thought it desirable to grant monopolies for new inventions only for a time, "to make the benefit to the Commonwealth more general." Sometimes patents for new inventions hindered the advance of industry, as in the case of Sir Basil Brooke's steel monopoly, which was afterwards annulled and superseded by the grant of a new patent to a Frenchman.

Another writer denounces monopolies, "which invade the liberty of the land, and intrench on the native commodities of the kingdom." Roger Coke went farther than these writers in the direction of freedom of trade. "Nothing is worse resented in our parliaments, or in ordinary discourse, than monopolies, and that deservedly; for they render the industry and ingenuity of many people useless, and the improvement of any new invention for the public more difficult, whilst the monopolists do things dearer and worse. I wish that encouragement were given to inventors of any beneficial mystery any other way than by patent of the sole use for fourteen years; for by that means the use of it becomes less and dearer to us, and may be more useful and cheaper to other nations who do not monopolize it, whereby they may enjoy more benefit by it than can be hoped for by us." Coke would grant monopolies in the case of luxuries—*e. g.* "French wines and brandies, Italian and Spanish wines and fruits, and all sorts of fine linen, lace, ribbons," etc., on the ground that they "impoverish and debauch the nation, and should therefore be driven by a few." Many of the commodities classed by Coke under the head of luxuries have since become necessaries.

The agitation against the monopolies shows that, although public opinion at this time was in the main favourable to restrictions on free enterprise, there was yet a large class who regarded with hostility the protective policy of the Middle Ages and attempts to force industry into artificial channels. The agitation led to the development of patent law, and the separation of inventions from the practice of the ordinary arts already known. After a long struggle the principle was established that no one should monopolize for private gain what was the equal right of all English citizens and necessary for general prosperity. The Statute of Monopolies was thus a move in the direction of free trade. But important as it was in this respect, it was no less important in another point of view, for it restricted the royal prerogative in the regulation of trade, and paved the way for the wider sanction of a representative Parliament.

CHAPTER II.

THE MONOPOLIES AND MODERN INDUSTRIAL CHANGES.

THE history of the monopolies throws light on the conditions of industry in the seventeenth century. Let us take one or two examples. At the beginning of the seventeenth century, the principal iron-fields of England were Sussex, Kent, and Surrey, Monmouth, and the Forest of Dean, while the industry was rising into importance in Nottinghamshire, Staffordshire, and Yorkshire. The best iron was imported from Spain. In 1612, Simon Sturtevant estimates the number of ironworks, including furnaces and forges, at 800; the iron was smelted with charcoal; the average weekly output from each furnace was fifteen tons of pigs, and from each forge three tons of iron bars. Two loads of charcoal, to the preparation of which four loads of wood were necessary, were consumed in the production of a ton of pigs, and three loads of charcoal were allowed for each ton of iron bars.

It is, therefore, not surprising that public attention was drawn to the effect of the iron trade on the woods and forests. Several statutes were passed restraining the building of furnaces, and attempts were made to encourage the growth of woods. Malynes complains that timber was advanced in price in consequence of the decay of the woods which were "consumed for manufactures besides sea cole." He also notices the use of coal in Germany for smelting iron. Simon Sturtevant, who obtained a patent in 1612, was the first Englishman to smelt iron with pit-coal. He contended that his method would stop the decay of woods, cheapen production, and revive and extend the iron manufacture. He said that by his invention, the annual charge of £500 per furnace, for charcoal, would be reduced to £30, £40, or at most £50. His process was unsuccessful, and he was followed by John Robinson, Gombleton, who erected his iron-works at Lambeth, and Dr. Jordan, but none of them obtained satisfactory results.

Dudley was acquainted with these experiments, and he had "former knowledge and delight in iron-works of his father's, when he was but a youth." In 1619 (*aet.* 19), he left Balliol College to assume the management of his father's iron-works at Pensnett, in Worcestershire. Here the scarcity of wood and charcoal led him to attempt the use of pit-coal. "I found such success at first tryal animated me, for at my tryal or blast, I made iron to profit with pit-coal, and found *Facere est addere Inventioni.*" The quality was good, but the quantity disappointing, for he could not produce more than three tons a week.

Very soon, however, he increased his weekly output to seven tons. With the influence of Lord Dudley he secured a patent, but during the whole of his life he suffered much in applying his invention. His iron-works were destroyed by the floods. The other iron-masters, afraid of being undersold, opposed him in every possible way. His prices were, for pigs, £4 a ton, and for bar iron £12, while the corresponding prices for iron produced by the old methods were £6 and £7, and £15 to £18. The iron-masters petitioned the King, and endeavoured to bring his invention under the Statute of Monopolies. Lord Dudley's influence, however, was too strong, and it was excepted from the operation of the Act. Dudley was turned out of his iron-works, but erected new furnaces at Sedgeley, where he also discovered new coal-mines. After developing these, he was turned out by violence, and his bellows cut by rioters. He obtained a new patent in 1632, and took as partners several persons with influence at Court, for his protection. But the opposition to him was renewed, his partners died, he himself was swindled, and during the Civil Wars his estate was sold. On the Restoration he failed to get his patent renewed, though he petitioned for it.

Though such small results attended the efforts of Dudley and the other inventors of the seventeenth century, they prepared the way for the great changes of the eighteenth. The iron trade of Sussex, Kent, and Surrey gradually flickered out as the supply of wood diminished, though furnaces were to be found there as late as the reign of Anne. The iron trade migrated to the coal-fields of Monmouth, Forest of Dean, and South Staffordshire. The reasons for this are plain. Though iron-ore was still smelted and made into bars by the old methods, yet "in all these countries now named there is an infinite of pit-coals, and the pit-coals being near the iron, and the iron-stone growing with the coals, there it is manufactured very cheap. . . . There never will be any want of pit-coals to work and manufacture the iron when once made into bars." So wrote Andrew Yarranton in 1677, the author of an interesting pamphlet, *England's Improvement*, in which he undertook to show "how to treat the Dutch without fighting, how to pay debts without money, and how to set at work all the poor of England." Yarranton said that the woods were not worth cutting, because coal was so cheap. He considered the woollen trade and the iron trade of equal importance, and was of opinion that woods should be specially preserved in the Forest of Dean to prevent the decay of the latter. Yarranton apparently knew nothing of Dudley's invention and the attempts made to apply it. They were known, however, to Henry Powle, who wrote an account of the iron trade in the same year (1677). According to Powle, the timber was then almost totally destroyed by the increase of the iron-works. Most of the inhabitants in the Forest of Dean were engaged in the iron trade. They found plenty of coal and iron-ore, and in some places red and yellow ochre. The best ore, brush-ore as they called it, was of a bluish colour, "very ponderous, and full of little shining specks, like grains of silver." This afforded the greatest quantity of iron; but it produced a metal "very soft and brittle," and therefore unfit for common use. To remedy this defect, they mixed it with another sort, which they called "their cinder." This was said to be "the rough and offal, thrown by in the Romans' time." The improved bellows driven by a water-wheel, which had superseded the old foot-blast, enabled them to extract the ore. The "sow" iron, made from the Roman cinders, being "of a most gentle, pliable, and soft nature, was easily and quickly to be wrought into manufactures." It was sent up the Severn to the forges of Worcestershire and Staffordshire. It then found its way to the workshops of "Stourbridge, Dudley, Wolverhampton, Sedgeley, Walsall, and of Birmingham," where it was manufactured into those hardware goods for which even then the district was becoming famous.

There were others, as well as Dudley, who had an inkl of the great future before the country when its vast mine resources came to be developed; and if the changes of tl period were dwarfed by the more rapid movement of t eighteenth century, we must remember that the true signi cance of such changes cannot be measured by their immedia results. These pioneers of the seventeenth century we: preparing the way for the greatest revolution of sentimen opinion, and material conditions which the Western Worl has ever seen.

The history of the nail trade during the last 300 year. shows in a very interesting manner the gradual evolution o: the modern industrial system. Before the sixteenth century, nail-making was merely a branch of the smith's handicraft. The nails were forged out of roughly-prepared rods or bars, a process which involved great waste of material. Towards the end of the sixteenth century the industry became localized in Staffordshire, Worcestershire, and part of Salop. The separation of the industry from the ordinary craft of the blacksmith was probably due to the introduction of "slitting mills," by Shutz, a German, who came to England in 1565. Slitting mills were also set up at Stanbridge in 1600, which supplied the nailers with raw material in the form of slit rods. There was an attempt to regulate the trade by statute in 1584-5, when a Bill was introduced to make nailing a separate employment in the counties above-mentioned. None but those apprenticed and trained to it were to practise it, and no apprentice was to set up a shop as a nailer unless he was thirty years old or married. Every nailer having two apprentices was to have also one journeyman. This Bill was read a first time, and rejected "upon the question." Early indications are found of the prevalence of the abuses which seem to have always existed in this industry. In 1604 it was said that carriers who carried iron from one part of the country to another bought up the unwrought iron, and thereby compelled the artificers to sell their iron wares not for money, but for unwrought iron, and even for other goods, such as corn, etc. These practices were forbidden in a Bill, which did not get further than the first reading. In 1606, Sir Bevis Bulmer took out a patent "for cutting and making of iron into small bars for rods to serve for the making of nails." This invention apparently did not succeed, but Clement Daubeney took it up, and improved upon it, and in 1618 obtained a patent. In 1678 there was an invention by Thomas Harvey which indicated a further change in the nail trade—the separation of nut and bolt making from the parent stock, though we do not know how far it was applied. Nail-making, which included the manufacture of nuts, bolts, rivets, and screws, was purely a domestic industry in all its branches until the end of the eighteenth century. The condition of the nailers, however, was never prosperous. In an *Essay to enable the Necessitous Poor to pay Taxes* (1713), it was stated that nailers worked from 4 a.m. on Monday till late on Saturday for 3*s.* per week, that sum being frequently reduced by the bad iron supplied. The remedy suggested was an extra allowance of 6*d.* on every 1000 nails, to be apportioned as follows—2*d.* to the nailer; 1*d.* for the school-master, school-books, and clothes for the nailer and his children, "to educate them to read their Bible, and to write, that they may do their duty towards God and man, and that they may know themselves"; 1*d.* to the wholesale dealer; and 2*d.* to the Corporation of Mines.

William Hutton has left an interesting description of the nailers thirty years after this period. There were few nail-makers left in the town (Birmingham). "Our nailers are chiefly masters, and rather opulent. The manufacturers are so scattered round the country, that we cannot travel far, in any direction, out of the sound of the nail hammer. But Birmingham, like a powerful magnet, draws the produce of the anvil to herself. When I first approached her, from Walsall, in 1741, I was surprised at the prodigious number of blacksmiths' shops upon the road; and could not conceive how a country, though populous, could support so many people of the same occupation. In some of these shops I observed one or more females, stript of their upper garment, and not overcharged with the lower, wielding the hammer with all the grace of the sex. . . . Struck with the novelty, I enquired, 'Whether the ladies in this country shod horses?' but was answered, with a smile, 'They are nailers.' A fire without heat, a nailer of a fair complexion, or one who despises the tankard, are equally rare amongst them. . . . While the master reaps the harvest of plenty, the workman submits to the scanty gleanings of penury, a thin habit, an early old age, and a figure bending towards the earth. Plenty comes not near his dwelling, except of rags, and of children. But few recruits arise from his nail-shop, except for the army. His hammer is worn into deep hollows, fitting the fingers of a dark and plump hand, hard as the timber it wears. His face, like the moon, is often seen through a cloud."

It will be instructive to indicate the relation between these changes and the present condition of the nail trade. In the sixteenth century it became separated from the blacksmith's craft. During the seventeenth century the trade was still further specialized, but included the group of small industries comprised under nails, nuts, bolts, rivets, and screws, all carried on under the domestic system. Then a further change took place. Screw-making was organized on the factory system. The process began in 1760, when there was an invention which appears to have gradually superseded the old process of filing the screw-threads on short wire cuttings. But little progress was made. Screws to drive into wood were made at Burton-on-Trent before 1798, by Messrs. Shorthouse, Wood and Co., the blanks being forged out of iron wire, for which they paid Messrs. Lloyd and Romwell's forges about £500 per annum. Thirty people were employed in screw-making. The same firm also made screws at Tettenhall and Hartshorn, in Derbyshire, where they employed fifty-nine people, and made 1,200 gross per week, by means of thirty-six engines or lathes, turned by one water-wheel. Each lathe cut "with great velocity" eight or nine screws a minute, and was stopped eighteen times in that short period to put in and take out the screw. The screws were of various sizes, weighing from half an ounce to thirty pounds per gross. Children could earn by the employment from 1*s.* 6*d.* to 1*s.* 9*d.* per week. It is said that before the war iron screws could not be made fast enough for exportation. But screw-making on the factory system did not show much progress until Whitworth's inventions in 1840. The other members of the nailing group also resisted the change of system, although there were upwards of a hundred more or less important inventions in these industries between 1760 and 1841. In 1861 the domestic system was still practically universal, except in the screw trade, which had passed finally under the new system. The next ten or eighteen years were very fertile in inventions affecting the various branches of the nail trade. The nut and bolt trade now became a machine industry; and although there are still in the district where it is carried on between twelve and twenty domestic workshops, the trade is practically organized on the factory system. Also, nearly all the nails now used can be made by machinery, so that the transition in this ancient branch of the blacksmith's craft is almost complete. It is interesting to notice that the inventions which have brought about this transformation cover a period of more than 400 years, and that the manufacture of nails by the ordinary blacksmith lingered on until quite recently, a relic of the past surrounded with the modern improvements, and may probably be still found in country villages.

Now this brief notice of the changes in one important group of industries indicates the point of view in which present forms of industrial organization should be considered if their good and evil is to be rightly estimated. We cannot, for example, understand the present condition of factory women in this group of hardware trades by merely concentrating attention on the phenomena of the last few years. It is necessary to take a long period of time. The condition of the women in nut and bolt or screw factories should be compared, not with that of textile workers, but with their prospects and condition in the domestic workshops, which factories have displaced and are displacing, if we wish to estimate the gain or loss of the modern system of industry. Society, as it were, had to choose between two forms of industrial organization, exhibiting in some respects opposite tendencies. We do not know to what extent women and children were employed in this industry in its early stages, but for many years previous to the introduction of the factory system, it was their principal sphere of employment in the hardware trades of the Black Country, and the evidence seems to indicate that no great changes had taken place from the seventeenth century to 1833, or even 1860. There is no doubt but that most of the evils exposed in the Reports of the Children's Employment Commission were very ancient. But the displacement of man's labour by that of women in the heavier branches of the trade may probably be traced to the competition of the machine-made nails, and the gradual restriction of the wrought nail trade to a few varieties. It is in an industry like this, carried on in small workshops, and beyond the reach of the factory inspector, that the evils of the employment of women and children are seen in their severest form. Here the middleman is supreme, and the truck system lingers on. Members of the same family cut down each other's wages to starvation point, while the isolation of the workers, and the want of corporate action or common aims, renders a strong trade union impossible. Unhealthy workshops and hard physical toil undermine the health, while the indiscriminate association of men and women weakens the moral character of the workers. The long hours of labour, and the opposition of interests between parents and children, sap the family life, and make economical management of the household and care for the young impossible. The transition to the factory system has increased the hardships of those who still cling to the wrought nail trade, but the factory hands are better off, and enjoy even greater freedom than was possible under the old system. There is not the same tendency towards the displacement of male labour. In the screw trade there was at one time (1851—1861) a more or less rapid increase in the number of young children and women, while the proportion of men employed fell off. But in the following ten years the tendency was reversed, and it is probable that the hardware trades organized on the factory system will not in the future be a promising sphere for the employment of women. In the nut and bolt trade, a more recent development in a district where domestic workshops were formerly universal, it is noteworthy that, while in the wrought nail trade women of all ages are employed, married and unmarried, there is a growing sentiment in favour of deserting the factory when the duties of married life are undertaken. Not more than 3 per cent. of the women employed in the nut and bolt factories are married, while from 63 to 65 per cent. are between fifteen and twenty-five years of age. The women now employed in the factories would, a generation ago, have found work in the nail shops or the nut and bolt shops, which have become nearly extinct. Comparing their prospects under the two systems, there is no single point in which factory organization has not led to an improvement. There are evils to be removed. There is reason to think that some features of the sweating system still survive. Two of the processes performed by the women, viz. *fraying* and *turning*, are too severe a strain on their physical strength. The rate of wages, 7*s.* per week on an average, is low compared with that in the textile industries. Trade Union efforts have not hitherto met with success, even if they have been made. But the healthier surroundings, the relatively higher wages, the less laborious work, and the more usual withdrawal of married women from the factories have already exercised a beneficial influence on the people. These causes, taken in conjunction with the rapid development of interest in municipal affairs, the improved sanitation, the growth of free libraries and other means of education, the more frequent gatherings of the people for social and political purposes, have greatly improved the lot of working men and women, who a few years ago had before them no better prospect than the domestic workshop could afford. These little Black Country towns still appear poor and dreary enough to the casual visitor. But within the last twenty years the change has been great. There is comfort, hopefulness, even enthusiasm, and a very active public spirit, where these characteristics formerly did not exist.

We have dwelt on the changes in this one group of industries because they illustrate the good and evil of the modifications of the last two hundred years, independent of phenomena, traceable in a great measure to the exceptional circumstances of 1791—1825. They supply a corrective to the vivid impressions of the industrial revolution conveyed by some highly-coloured accounts of it. In this group of industries the factory system has helped to remove evils which grew up during the seventeenth century. We shall see in a later chapter that those evils were not peculiar to the hardware industries of the Black Country, but were found in other branches of the iron trade, in the textile and other industries. We shall there resume a discussion suggested by the Patent Lists, which contain the record of the most important changes since the beginning of the seventeenth century, and enable us to connect those changes with the more recent movements of our own time.

CHAPTER III.

THE TRADING COMPANIES.

§ 1. *Extent of their Organization.*

WE must now examine the constitution and policy of the great trading companies, which were formed during the sixteenth and the seventeenth centuries for extending foreign trade, and which enjoyed a monopoly against all outsiders. Their influence in seventeenth century commerce was as far-reaching as that of the gilds, in home trade, during the Middle Ages. A merchant who wished to engage in foreign enterprise had little chance of success unless he became a member of one of the great companies. If he did not take this step, he was looked upon with as much suspicion and dislike by the commercial world as the modern Trade Union feels for the "blackleg," while he did not enjoy any of the privileges and immunities of that much abused industrial agent. For the companies had extensive powers of fine and imprisonment, and could bring the influence of the law to bear upon the private trader who would not submit to their regulations, in a manner quite alien to English law and custom at the present time. There are few passages in English commercial history more interesting than the records of the attempts made by the private trader to break down the monopoly of the trading companies; and none which exhibit so clearly the evil tendencies of this type of organization.

There is some analogy between a modern railway company and a trading company of the seventeenth century, though the one performs different functions, and has not such extensive powers and privileges as the other enjoyed. If we imagine the principles of railway organization extended to the whole foreign trade of the country at the present time, we can get some idea of the form which commercial enterprise would assume if the old methods of organization were applied. Let us picture the condition of things at the beginning of the reign of James I. The Russia Company had the monopoly of the trade to Russia, Armenia, Media, Hyrcania, Persia, and the Caspian Sea. The trade to Norway, Sweden, and the Baltic was under the control of the Eastland merchants. The Merchant Adventurers enjoyed the monopoly of the trade from the Cattegat to the mouth of the Somme. Then came the Levant Company with its monopoly of the trade of the Mediterranean and the East. In the newly-discovered lands, the Guinea Company traded to the West Coast of Africa, while the East India Company's charter included the islands and continents beyond the Cape to the Straits of Magellan. In North America, the South Virginia Company monopolized the trade of Maryland, Virginia, and Carolina; and the Plymouth Adventurers Pennsylvania, New Jersey, New York, and New England. Here and there bodies of merchants had rights which infringed the charters of these companies — *e. g.*, the Hull merchants were protected against the Muscovy Company; Sir Edward Michelborne and others had privileges against the East India Company;

while private traders might have been found over the whole field trying their best to break down the monopolies; but the French trade was the only one free and open to all Englishmen. Thus the study of the foreign trade of England in the seventeenth century is practically the study of the constitution, policy, and influence of the trading associations.

Nor is the subject interesting only from this point of view. Throughout the century controversy raged about certain aspects of the trading companies in much the same manner as we are now deluged with articles for and against the socialistic tendencies of the age. Gradually men began to have more precise notions on economic theory, on the balance of trade, the relations of Government to industry and commerce, and on freedom of trade. The subject falls into its place also in the political development of the British Empire and the United States. From the early operations of the East India Company has grown the English empire in the East; and Professor Bryce has pointed out the traces of the old charters given to the trading companies in the State constitutions of America.

The student of modern economic questions cannot neglect the experience of 200 years of commercial history. The character and the policy of the trading companies in dealing with the difficulties of their own age supply many suggestions capable of application in our own day, and when their experience cannot be utilized, it sometimes indicates the pitfalls which we may avoid. How far was foreign trade really fostered by entrusting its management to close corporations? Were their charters the mere reflex of public opinion of the time, or did there exist a body of opinion hostile to their formation? Was the close relation between Government and industry beneficial to the community as a whole, or did that relation foster a system of corruption and lower the standard of public life? Did the company organization retard or encourage individual enterprise? Lastly, how did the companies and the controversies raised by them assist in the development of economic theory? These are some of the questions which the following pages will enable us to answer.

§ 2. *Character of the Trading Companies.*

Their monopoly had a political rather than an economical basis. In the remote countries to which the merchants resorted to open up new trades, there was very often either no central government at all which could secure justice and upright dealing between rival traders, and put an end to their disputes; or the native governments were too weak and disorganized to protect the interests of the merchants or prevent themselves from becoming the prey of the competitors for their trade. Nor was the home government associated in the minds of the traders with that all-pervading spirit of law and justice which has become or is becoming deeply rooted in civilized nations. The countenance or aid of the Government was invoked as some external force to be persuaded, cajoled, or bribed into helping one section of the community against all others, rather than the impartial arbiter between conflicting interests, acting for the benefit of all. The Government, on the other hand, did not assume full responsibility in the commercial dealings of this country with others, but delegated many of its functions to the trading companies. Their organization, in its early days, was necessary for the protection of merchants while engaged in trade; and, when new lands were discovered, or new connections formed with Eastern countries, the sphere in which such protection was necessary was widened. The Company in its corporate capacity became the central authority to which, through its officials, the individual trader could appeal when disputes or difficulties arose. In the leading ports to which they traded, the Companies had their consuls and agents, who could watch over the interests of their members, and see that agreements were adhered to. The Companies paid the expenses of this official establishment, and it was natural that they should have the right of appointing the consuls and ambassadors. If, again, it was in the interests of the individual merchant that there should exist a strong corporate body able to extend to him countenance and protection, it was no less due to the Company that all traders to the places in which they were responsible should be amenable to its authority, and should contribute to the expenses of its establishment. It would have been just as fair to excuse the ordinary citizen from paying taxes, and to place him beyond the operation of the law, while all other privileges of citizenship were freely granted to him, as to allow the "interloper" to enjoy the privileges and profits of foreign trade without sharing the responsibility and without becoming a member of the Company, which had won and maintained whatever rights the trader possessed. When the Government assumed the responsibility, appointed the consuls and ambassadors, and paid the expenses out of the general taxes of the State, then the need for the company organization passed away, and all English subjects might be allowed to trade freely, subject only to the law of the land. Until then it was inevitable that extensive powers should be granted to the trading companies, for in foreign lands they stood in the same relation to the individual merchant as the State. The trading company was, in fact, relative to the English Parliament, in the same position as a colonial government, so far as trade was concerned.

So far we have spoken of the trading companies as if all of them conformed to one type of organization. The observations we have made are indeed applicable to all alike, but the degree in which abuses crept into the system depended largely on their internal organization. They were, broadly speaking, of two kinds—(1) regulated, (2) joint stock companies, and throughout the seventeenth century there was much controversy as to the relative merits of the two principles. It will be easily seen that the former, which was also the more ancient, was more favourable to individual enterprise than the latter, though experience proved that the organization of the regulated company might be so worked as to become virtually a monopoly of the most pronounced type. The "regulated" principle was that every trader, upon paying certain fees and submitting to the rules and bye-laws of the Company, should trade with his own capital, at his own risk, for whatever amount he chose, without reference to the Company in its corporate capacity. All members who had paid a certain amount in duties were entitled to vote at the general courts, when the regulations were settled, in accordance with which the trade was to be carried on. In the case of the joint stock companies, on the other hand, the individual trader became merged in the corporation, and shared in the common profit and loss. To understand the controversies between the respective champions of these two principles, we must give a more detailed account of the principal trading companies.

§ 3. *The Free Trade Bills* (1604).

Let us take first the Free Trade Bills of 1604, which were directed against all the existing trading companies, though it appears that the Merchant Adventurers aroused the strongest opposition. Without dissolving any company, the bills abrogated all orders tending to monopoly. They abolished apprenticeship as a qualification for membership, and gave free access to all men. Provision was made for necessary contributions to public charges, and, to meet the objection that the existence of the companies was necessary for the maintenance of ambassadors, consuls, and agents, and for giving costly presents, it was provided that the trading merchants should contribute to these charges. There was a further provision that people should not go out of the realm "but for their present traffic." The committee, of which Sir Edwin Sandys was chairman, sat five whole afternoons upon these Bills, and interviewed both sides. Counsel was heard for the Bills, and several of the principal Aldermen of London against them. We are told, that of the London merchants three-fourths joined in the complaint against the remaining fourth, and of this fourth "some standing stiffly for their own company, yet repined at other companies." It was urged that, while there were 5000 or 6000 persons, counting children and apprentices, free of the companies, yet the practical tendency of the present system was to throw the bulk of the trade into the hands of some 200 persons. This was "*against the natural right and liberty of the subjects of England*," and it was maintained that the law was on the side of the free traders, who pointed to the example of other countries, and especially Holland, whose trade flourished without restraint. It was said that freedom of trade would lead to the increase of wealth and shipping, *the more equal distribution of wealth*, and the increase of revenue. Further, it was urged that, while war might have justified the existence of the companies in times past, yet now, with a prospect of peace, they were no longer necessary. If trade were free, they looked to an extension of commerce beyond its present limits. The provisions of the Bills cut the ground from beneath the Opposition, whose arguments were of the feeblest description. It was urged that there was monopoly only when the liberty of trade was confined to one man, that the Bills were an injury to those who had served their apprenticeship, and that if trade were free, the rich would "eat out the poor, who were not able to sell at the instant, to make themselves savers, and so there would grow a monopoly *ex facto*." To which it was replied: "This reason showeth thus much, that a crafty head, with a greedy heart and a rich purse, is able to take advantage of the need of his neighbour, which no man doubteth of." The Merchant Adventurers pleaded their ancient services; but, while these were acknowledged, it was said that this Company, being the spring of all monopolies, deserved least favour. "In sum the Bill was a good Bill, though not in all points, perhaps, so perfect as it might be; while defects might be soon remedied and supplied in future Parliaments." We are told that at the third reading the Bill was three days debated, and "passed with great consent and applause of the House (as being for the exceeding benefit of all the land), scarce forty voices dissenting from it." It was thrown out by the Lords.

§ 4. *Formation of the Russia Company.*

The history of the Russia Company is as instructive as this parliamentary incident. The Russia Company took its origin in an association known as the "Merchant Adventurers of England for the discovery of lands and territories unknown." The object of the association was strictly commercial. The merchants who formed it desired to rival Spain and Portugal in extending their trade to distant countries. In 1553, a capital of £6000 was subscribed, in 240 shares of £25 each, and Sir Hugh Willoughby was sent out to look for the north-west passage. The unfortunate issue of the voyage is well known. The Company obtained its first charter from Queen Mary in 1555, when Sebastian Cabot was made governor, and a Board of Direction established, consisting of four consuls and twenty-four assistants, chosen from "the most sad, discreet, and honest of the said fellowship." The new Company had very extensive privileges. They might acquire lands, impose forfeitures on offenders against their privileges, levy taxes on members, and make conquests. They had the monopoly of the trade with Russia, and with any other country discovered by them. The Czar, Ivan the Terrible, was fully alive to the value of this new means of communication with the Western world. On their second venture, when they sailed in two ships up the Dwina to Vologda, and proceeded thence on sledges to Moscow, he granted the Company freedom of resort to any of his dominions, and other privileges; while, on the other hand, the Company took every advantage of their position, and endeavoured to open up a new route to Persia for raw silk, and to discover a north-east passage. In 1556, the Company was sanctioned by Act of Parliament, with the name, the "Fellowship of English Merchants for the discovery of New Trades." The Company had the monopoly of the trade to Russia, Armenia, Media, Hyrcania, Persia, and the Caspian Sea, with certain important exceptions. The fishery trade on the coasts of Norway was left open. A special clause was introduced in favour of the merchants of York, Newcastle, Hull, and Boston, who might become members of the Company before December 25th, 1567. These merchants had for several years been engaged in the trade with Russia. Commerce was to be carried on in English ships with a majority of English sailors. (*Vide* Navigation Acts, 5 Rich. II. c. 3; 4 Hen. VII. c. 10; 32 Hen. VIII. c. 14; 1 Eliz. c. 13.) The interests of the English woollen manufacturers were guarded by a clause prohibiting the exportation of woollen cloths or kerseys, unless dressed and dyed in England.

§ 5. *Loss of their privileges.*

In the first years of its existence, favoured by the support of the Czar, the Russia Company rapidly developed its trade. They soon, however, began to experience difficulties when the Czar perceived that the hopes he cherished were not likely to be fulfilled. The trading advantages of his connection with England, great as they were, did not appeal to him so much as the hope of a political alliance. The new communication brought him into contact with the better methods of warfare practised in Europe; it supplied him with improved arms and ordnance. Not content with these benefits, he desired an alliance with England, and he looked to that country to afford him a refuge, if, as he had every reason to expect, he should be driven from his throne. Elizabeth, however, showed no disposition to encourage his political views. She confined herself in the various missions to his court to a discussion of strictly commercial relations, simply endeavoured to advance the interests of the new Company, and courteously ignored all representations made to her of a more political character. Disappointed in his hopes of bringing about the alliance with England, the Czar turned against the Company. In 1571 their privileges were suspended, but were soon after restored through the instrumentality of Mr. Jenkinson. Difficulties again arose and fresh negotiations were opened, but the Company did not regain their old position, and at the end of the sixteenth century the trade was greatly decayed. There were other reasons, however, for the decay of their trade, an examination of which reveals some of the vices of this form of monopoly. The Company soon ceased to include within it even the majority of those who were engaged in the trade. In 1555 there were 207 members, fifty years later this number had diminished to 160, and, in 1654, that is, one hundred years after its incorporation, there were only 55 members. The report of the Committee on the Free Trade Bills introduced to the House of Commons in 1604, complained that the directors limited the proportion of stock held by individual members, made "one purse and common stock," consigned their goods to one agent at Moscow, and on the return voyage to one agent in London, through whom they disposed of all imported commodities, and then rendered what account they pleased. "This was a strong and shameful monopoly, both abroad and at home." They accused the Company of trying to cause an artificial scarcity of Russian commodities by restricting the supply. The price of cordage had risen within a very short period 150 per cent., and the Company had contracted with their buyers to bring no more of that commodity for three years. It was contended that the Company by this selfish and short-sighted policy had ruined their trade. Unable to compete with the Dutch and Hamburgers, who were vigorous and eager to seize every opportunity of ousting the English traders, hampered by no restrictions on their trade with Russia, with low freights, low cost of transport and ships better adapted to the trade, the English merchants were driven from the Russian markets. Moreover, private traders saw that the returns were quicker, and that it paid them better to make common cause with the Dutch in their competition with the Muscovy Company. We know that the latter had no more malignant enemies in Russia than the English interlopers. From its first formation, a section of the commercial world looked with disfavour on their exclusive privileges. The interlopers had taken advantage of the fact that Narva, which was captured in 1558, was not included in Russian territory when the first charter was granted, and on that pretext had opened up a trade, maintaining that by doing so they infringed no monopoly. They obtained special privileges from the Czar, in defiance of the Company's charter, and endeavoured in various ways to frustrate the negotiations of their representative. In the first years of the Company's existence, there was, no doubt, good reason for confining the trade to its early pioneers. They had been subjected to great expense, they had opened up communications with Russia at great risk, and their losses had been considerable. It was natural to grant them exclusive rights until they were re-imbursed, and they had a strong case against the interlopers who wished to step in and snatch the fruits of their enterprise. But such rights would have received full satisfaction had the monopoly been granted only for a term of years. There was no reason why the trade should be confined, after the original members were dead, to London merchants, who shared none of the perils of the first undertakings. Private adventurers were fully justified in their efforts to break down the monopoly of a company which no longer encouraged but prevented the development of trade, and which imposed vexatious restrictions on the free enterprise of English merchants.

§ 6. *The Whale Fishery.*

The history of the whale fishery clearly exhibits the policy pursued during the seventeenth century. The importance of the fishing trade as a nursery for mariners was early recognized; and many attempts were made to give legislative aid to its development. It was to be expected, therefore, that when the trade to Archangel acquainted the English with the whale fisheries of the northern seas, there should be much competition for the trade. The Biscayners and Norwegians had engaged in the fishing at an early date, and the East India Company claimed the credit of first employing them in their interests. They discovered Greenland, and taught the English how to kill whales. We have seen that a proviso was inserted in the charter of the Russia Company in favour of the merchants of Newcastle, York, Hull, and Boston, who had for many years pushed their trade to the northern seas, and their interest in the whale fishery no doubt grew out of these voyages.

In 1598 we find the Russia Company commencing the Spitzbergen fishery, of which they secured the monopoly in 1613. The joint efforts of the Russia and East India

Companies, early in the seventeenth century, to discover a north-west passage, gave a stimulus to the trade. Several expeditions were sent out, and though they failed in the attainment of their immediate object, they rendered valuable service by prosecuting the whale fishing. Thus there were two sections of English struggling for the monopoly of the trade—the Russia and East India Companies, who made common cause, and the merchants of Hull and York. For several years these were left to fight it out. But, in 1612, a rival appeared in the shape of the Dutch, and though on the first occasion the English plundered and threatened to confiscate their ships, they were not to be daunted. In 1614 they returned with eighteen vessels, of which four were ships of war, and fished in spite of the exclusive pretensions of the English Company. The enterprise of the Dutch in developing their fishing trade is shown by the pamphlets published about this time,—*e. g. England's Way to Win Wealth*, by Tobias Gentleman, in 1614, *The Trades' Increase* (1615), *The Defence of Trade* (1615), by Sir Dudley Digges, etc.,—in which their prosperity was attributed to this source alone. The Dutch themselves regarded their fishing, carried on mainly in English waters, as "their chiefest trade." They were, therefore, not likely to suffer the English to monopolize the whale fishery. We shall see presently, that their efforts were so successful that they drove the English from the trade. In 1618 the Danes had thrust themselves in between the English and the Dutch, and claimed the exclusive right to Greenland. In spite of their more powerful rivals, the Russia Company continued to struggle. for the English monopoly. They were beaten in a dispute with Hull for the possession for the Isle of Trinity, but they were influential enough to crush a new Scotch Company which had been chartered by James I.

In the following year, 1619, they again joined with the East India Company in a whaling expedition, but after several unfortunate voyages, both Companies retired from the trade. The finances, indeed, of the Russia Company at this time appear to have been very low. When the Scotch charter, alluded to above, was revoked, the Company was bound to compensate several people for the losses they had sustained, but three years afterwards no steps whatever had been taken to fulfil these claims, and the Company stooped even to the meanest practices to escape its responsibility. It appears from various petitions that the Company was heavily in debt, and unable to satisfy its creditors. The study of its affairs at this time shows not only its financial difficulties, but also how difficult it was for a poor client to obtain redress from a powerful corporation. Mary Brocas claimed £1000, which she had lent to the Company, on January 3rd, 1617, at 8 per cent. The interest had been paid for a time, but the Company soon stopped payment, and did not return the principal. Legal proceedings had been stayed on the pretext that an Order in Council, October 19th, 1621, protected them from such claims. The Committee of the Lords, after examining the case (May 27th, 1624), ordered the Company to bring to their Treasurer, by Midsummer Day, all the levies and assessments made for the payment of their principal debts, owing to strangers, not free of the Company, who had lent their money. Mary Brocas was to be first paid, with interest at 5 per cent. for the period which had elapsed since the Company had stopped payment. More than twelve months afterwards (August 5th,

1625), she had received only £700, and she complained that the Company was attempting to evade the order of May 27th, 1624. So terrible were the scourges of the plague in London at this time, that the Lords thought it dangerous to bring the governor and directors to town, and so they ordered the petitioner's cause to be referred to the Court of Chancery, "to be executed according to the former order, with as much conveniency as may be, in respect of the sickness at this time." In the following year, they dealt with her case along with the other creditors of the Company; but on June 19th, 1628, the Committee reported that the order of May 27th, 1624, was in no way performed, and that the Company was attempting to defraud its creditors of their debts. The governor and directors were told that they deserved severe punishment for their contempt of the Orders of the House, upon which they desired that the accounts might be audited. The audit revealed "the gross juggling of the Company to defraud their creditors." The Lords made stringent orders for the payment of their debts, but we are not told whether they were carried out, and we do not know whether Mrs. Mary Brocas, after her ten years' struggle, succeeded in recovering her money from the clutches of the Muscovy merchants.

§ 7. *The Settlement of* 1654.

Deeply involved in debt as they were, and driven from many of their markets by the vigorous competition of the Dutch, the Company did not cease to fight their English rivals for the monopoly of the whale fishery. In 1653-4 we have several petitions on both sides. The Muscovy Company claimed to have discovered Greenland, and to have protected the trade from the violence of the Dutch, although, so far from protecting English interests against the Dutch, they had allowed the trade, through their mismanagement, inefficiency, and unwise policy, to fall into the hands of that nation. The Company took credit to themselves for importing fins, oil, formerly brought from Biscay, and declared that the orders of the Navy Committee of 1645, and of the Council of Trade in 1650, conferred upon them the monopoly of the trade. They adduced several plausible reasons to show that the only method which could be safely adopted for the management of the fishery was by a single company with a joint stock. The private adventurers, on the other hand, maintained that *they* had discovered the fishery forty years before, but the Company claimed the sole right thereto, on pretext of an Act of Parliament which had no relation to it. Under colour of Council Orders, the Company had suppressed or imprisoned all who were not of their number, thus monopolizing the trade, enhancing the price of oil, and compelling the importation of much Dutch oil. They now desired the confirmation of their claim to Horn Sound and Bell Sound, leaving the others free; but the ice made most of the latter inaccessible, and the two former were large enough for more fishers than ever had ventured thither. "Could it be consistent with public good to restrain the fishing to fifty people, who could not bring in sufficient oil, and who enhanced the price, when others offered to set out double the shipping if the trade were free? The adventurers had in that year sent out 1100 tons of shipping, which was as much as the Company's average; while if the Company's desires were granted, their voyages would be destroyed."

Some private adventurers, too weak perhaps to carry on the struggle, tried to make separate agreements with the Company. Mr. Horth, for example, proposed to have one-sixth of the harbours, on condition that he supplied one-sixth of the men and fishing. They, however, refused this offer, on the ground that if they made such an arrangement with one, they must admit others to a share in the trade on similar conditions. Others attempted a compromise. They saw that if they made common stock with the Company, as Horth proposed, they might ultimately be ruined; for the Company might find it to their advantage to engage in a few losing voyages, and so drive out the private traders, who had not sufficient capital to combat such a policy. Could not the Greenland harbours be thrown open, a limit being put upon the number allowed to fish there? It was at length proposed that the Company and the Hull traders should have two-thirds of the fishing, the remaining one-third being left to the private traders, and the fishery being managed by a committee.

These suggestions became the basis of a new settlement, and in April 1654, an Ordinance was passed for the constitution of a Committee of Management for the fishery, representing the Company, the Hull merchants, and the other interests involved. The whale fishery, however, did not prosper. Sir Francis Brewster, who collected much useful information, pointed out in 1702 the great decay of the trade since the reign of James I. His remarks were, he said, "not a random guess, but taken out of the several ports of the kingdom." "The Dutch and Hamburgers employ nearly 20,000 men in the Greenland fishing, and we not one." Such statements are not to be received as rigidly accurate, but they sufficiently indicate the severity of Dutch competition, which was no doubt aided by the dissensions amongst the different bodies of English merchants, who were all trying to secure a monopoly of the trade. De Witt says that since the Dutch-Greenland Company was dissolved, their whale fishery had increased in the ratio of 1 : 10; while Child points out that the Dutch trade to Russia and Greenland, where they had no companies, was forty times that of England.

§ 8. *Missions of William Prideaux and Lord Carlisle.*

While the Muscovy Company was engaged in these disputes, a new attempt was being made (1654) through the instrumentality of William Prideaux to revive their trade in Russia, which had fallen into decay. Since the last years of Charles I. the Company had been restricted to Archangel, and many of the privileges formerly enjoyed in the Czar's dominions had been withdrawn. The execution of Charles I. made the Czar hostile to the claims of the English merchants. This, however, was not the only nor even the principal reason for the decay of English trade in Russia at this time. Indeed, the privileges of the Company had been taken away before the execution of Charles. The cause of the depressed condition of their trade is to be found in their foolish attempts to keep up prices, and the competition of the Dutch, who undersold the English merchants. "Therefore, the taking away of their privileges came from themselves," said the Czar, in reply to Prideaux's request for their renewal. The English merchants were also charged with the non-fulfilment of a singular bargain, namely, to supply the Czar with all goods imported by them at their prices in England. As the Czar was the largest trader and manufacturer in his own dominions, this must have given him considerable advantage over his own subjects. It was said that the English merchants sold adulterated cloth, defrauded the customs, and brought in prohibited commodities. These charges were of course denied, and Prideaux ascribed them to the malice of the "malignant English." At any rate, true or false, they supplied the Czar with a pretext for merely expressing friendly intentions, and for postponing the decision on the object of Prideaux's mission until he had got rid of the war with Poland, when he hoped to have more leisure.

Lord Carlisle visited the Russian Court in 1663-4, and made another attempt to obtain a renewal of privileges, but he met with no better success than Prideaux, and the Company had to be re-organized. The old Joint Stock was done away with, and henceforward the merchants formed a regulated company. In this form, in which it was open to all who could pay the entrance fees and submit to the orders imposed by the governing body, the Company lingered on until the end of the eighteenth century.

The history of the Russia Company exhibits the gradual modification, in favour of the private adventurers, of rules designed to secure a monopoly. The peculiar circumstances which attended the opening up of Russia threw the monopoly of the trade into the hands of those of its discoverers who came most prominently before the commercial world, and who at the same time possessed enough influence at Court to obtain an exclusive charter. Other adventurers must, at any rate, have been early in the field. From the first days of the Company's existence, private traders tried to break down its monopoly. Aided by the competition of the Dutch, the financial weakness of the Company and its suicidal policy, the outsiders ultimately gained the victory; for they secured adequate representation on the Committee of Management of one of its most important northern trades, and the constitution was modified in a manner which ostensibly threw open the trade to all who desired to share in it.

§ 9. *The Levant or Turkey Company.*

A regulated company, however, could be so managed as to become a close monopoly. This will be illustrated by the history of the Levant Company. The English carried on a trade with the Barbary States as early as the reign of Henry VII., when ships from London, Bristol, and Southampton traded to Scio in the Levant. There is, however, little to chronicle until the voyage of Captain Bodenham to the Greek Archipelago in 1550; and direct commercial relations between England and Turkey date from the visit to Aleppo in 1553 of Anthony Jenkinson, who obtained the privilege of paying no more duties than the French and Venetians, and of being on the same footing as the most-favoured nation. But the English were indisposed to engage in the Levant trade; they were repelled by the dangers that awaited them in seas infested with pirates; and they were contented with the Turkish commodities with which Venice already supplied them. No further steps were taken for twenty-five years, when some merchants of London, with Edward Osborne as the leading spirit, began to develop the trade. In 1581, they obtained from Elizabeth Letters Patent for seven years, conferring a monopoly of the trade on the merchants who had been enterprising enough to embark in it, but reserving the right of revoking the charter upon one year's notice being given. It does not appear to have been renewed in 1588, and it is evident from the terms of the new charter of 1592, that, in the interval, others had been attracted into the trade. Three different sets of traders are mentioned, and the privileges are granted to fifty-three merchants for a period of twelve years. They were allowed to re-export Levant commodities without the payment of additional duties, and they had the monopoly of the trade to the Levant seas. There were, however, provisions for admitting other traders. The Levant Company now had a resident ambassador in Constantinople. That the post was one of difficulty and danger at that time is evident from the fate of Sir Edward Barton. The presence of Barton was a great advantage to the merchants, and the Christian population in general, to whom he rendered many services. But he aroused the hostility of the Turkish nobles, who procured his death by poison. His sister, Mary Lough, when trying in 1624 to obtain from the Company restitution of the ambassador's charges, said that the Turkish nobles feared the conversion of the Grand Signior to Christianity, through Barton's influence!

On the expiration of the twelve years, James I. substituted a perpetual charter for the terminable license which had been granted them. But the Company did not prosper. In 1606 they had a dispute with Southampton, to which Elizabeth had granted the exclusive privilege of importing the sweet wines of Malvoisie and Rhetimo. They became involved in debt, and suffered also from interlopers, who entered the trade without being duly qualified. An attempt was made to deal with the latter in an Ordinance of 1643, for upholding the monopoly of the Company. But they were to exclude no one willing to become a member of the

Company on payment of £50 if above 25, and £25 under that age.

In September 1653, the Company said there was "so great and almost total declination in their trade" that they were unable to maintain an ambassador at Constantinople. They hoped their affairs would improve after the treaty with Holland, and that their duties would increase sufficiently to extinguish their debts and support their charge.

§ 10. *Difficulties of the Turkey Company.*

The financial difficulties of the Company continued for many years. In 1705 their losses amounted to as much as £120,000. It is not sufficient to refer this decay of the Levant trade to those general causes which we are wont to associate with the restraints and prohibitions of the Mercantile System, and to include the Turkey Company in the general condemnation with which economists have treated that system. The decay of the trade was due to a concurrence of circumstances, which may be traced to the constitution and policy of the Company, the competition of rival associations, the heavy Turkish exactions, or other similar causes. One very important cause of the decay of their trade was the opening up of the new route to the East by the East India Company, who imported commodities formerly monopolized by the Turkey merchants at rates so low that it was impossible for the Levant Company to hold their own. They might have recovered from the effects of this competition, but later on the East India Company struck a heavier blow at their prosperity by supplanting them in the trade in raw silk, which they had brought in exchange for the woollen goods of England. This cause alone would account for the great diminution in their trade and influence. Along with the competition of a rival organization, the old route to Persia was stopped, and Russia diverted much of the trade which originally had fallen into their hands.

It was also alleged that changes in manufacturing processes had led to a diminution in the consumption of some of the commodities, such as galls and mohair yarn, which had formed an important branch of the Levant trade. With the eighteenth century, their difficulties were increased by the growing competition of the French, who availed themselves of the free port of Leghorn for the importation of Levant goods, and for venting their own wares. Their success was ascribed to their great resources in the American colonies—for example, indigo, sugar and coffee; and to the development of their fine woollen trade, in which they undersold the English Turkey merchants. The Company was ill-qualified to cope with these new conditions; the exportation of bullion was still forbidden, though the experience of the East India Company might have shown them how greatly this would hamper them in their commerce with the East; instead of trying by every legitimate means to attract more capital into their trade, to cheapen the cost of carriage, and to give every facility for the export of English goods, they engaged in that monopolizing policy which was the ruin of similar organizations.

Beyond the regulations necessary in those days when the trading associations had to discharge many of the duties which have since devolved upon the Government, the Turkey Company had given a wise liberty of trade to its individual members; and these characteristics frequently won the approbation of the more enlightened writers. But the tendency of a widely-extended organization is for the management to fall into the hands of the few energetic, interested people at the centre of affairs. Theoretically favourable, on the whole, to freedom of trade, the Turkey merchants strove to restrict the enterprise of the many in the interests of the London section. Their charter of 1661 directed that no person residing within twenty miles of London, except noblemen and gentlemen of quality, should be admitted into the Company, unless first made free of the City of London. The west country clothiers had to bring up their cloths to London before the Company would buy them, and they complained that the carriage rates to London equalled those to Turkey from Bristol and other western ports. Thus the Company allowed the trade to fall into the hands of the French, Dutch, and Venetians.

§ 11. *Methods of Securing their Monopoly.*

They further subjected their members to vexatious restraints in the exportation of their woollen goods in order to keep up prices in Turkey. The export trade to Turkey had been carried on sometimes with the private ships of members, sometimes with general ships, chartered by the Company in its corporate capacity. If there was unusual delay in the despatch of the latter, liberty was given to every member to export his goods in whatever manner he liked. From the conclusion of the war (1713) until 1717, there was an open trade—*i. e.* the members made their own arrangements without reference to the governing body, and the ships were sent in the autumn or at Christmas. The cloth ships had sailed for Turkey as usual at the end of 1717, and many members of the Company, expecting the trade to continue in the same manner, prepared their cargoes for the following year; but on March 26th, 1718, the Company decided that for the future members should trade only by general ships, which should depart at such times as they should be pleased to appoint. This order was followed by another a month later, when they resolved to levy a duty of 20 per cent. in Turkey on the cloth of any member who did not observe the former order, and added that the date of the departure of the general ships would be discussed on October 23rd following. The reason they alleged for this course was that it was intended to raise the value of English manufacture abroad and silk at home; "hereby evidently demonstrating their private advantage; that of the nation doubtless lying more in a large consume than in a large price." Many members thought these proceedings a great hardship, but acquiesced, in the expectation that, at least, they would be permitted to export their cloth in the Company's own way. But, on November 6th, they resolved to adjourn the further consideration of shipping for two months longer. From this it was evident that they intended no ships to sail that year. So a representation was made to the Ministry, and Mr. Secretary Craggs sent for the Company and desired them to reconsider the matter. This they did at a general court on December 4th, when they resolved that they would choose ships for the immediate exportation of cloth on January 8th following. But when January 8th arrived, instead of choosing ships, they ordered a report, to be presented on January 22nd. This measure of delay was carried by a majority of only one. The report was duly presented, whereupon they said they would in good time choose the ships, which were not to depart before July 1st next. This was understood to mean winter, which would have completed two years' prohibition of trade.

By this time the patience of the aggrieved merchants was exhausted, and they sought relief from Parliament. They said that the Company's charter did not warrant them in such a prohibition or restraint of trade; that it was illegal to levy 20 per cent. upon members' estates; and that such proceedings were not for the common good. To justify their action, the Company published extracts from letters sent by their consuls and agents at Constantinople, Aleppo, Smyrna, and other places, urging that the orders which had been issued were rendered necessary by the distressed condition of trade, for which a prohibition was the best remedy. The Company looked forward to an extension of their trade, if the supply of woollen goods were restrained for a year. Fifty-three members of the Company were found foolish enough or interested enough to issue a circular (February 3rd, 1718-19) giving their support to this policy. The Company maintained that they were strictly within their legal right in issuing the restraining orders. To which it was replied that their power of making bye-laws was not disputed, but they had thought fit to conceal the express proviso in their charter, that such bye-laws should not interfere with the rights of the individual trader. The absurdity of their arguments was pointed out, and it was maintained that they could not direct the method of lading and the time of departure of the ships unless the power was expressly conceded to them in their charter, while the evidence they had produced proved the necessity of a constant trade. A Bill was introduced into the House of Commons to deal with the matter, whereupon the Company gave notice that all restraint was removed, and would not be again imposed upon the members. Thus the delays which the influential London merchants were able to impose on the other members of the Company practically gave them a monopoly of the trade.

Another incident which took place at the same period shows the same tendency in their attempts to deal with the competition of other nations. When the Navigation Act was passed, a proviso was introduced to the effect that it should not extend to the commodities imported into Italy from the East Indies or elsewhere, or to bullion. The French took advantage of this clause, and were not only driving the Turkey Company from their markets abroad, but competed with them in their English trade. The Company therefore proposed that the clause should be repealed, which would have the effect of conferring upon them the monopoly of the supply of commodities which hitherto had been exempted from the operation of the Act. It was urged that this course would carry into effect the intention of the Act. The Company pointed to the success of the French; especially in that branch of the trade, in fine woollen goods, on which they could alone rely, for securing the raw silk of Turkey. They could not export bullion. How then could they vie with the French, who were alive to the importance of this as an aid in driving their trade? To the Italian merchants, who would be prejudiced if the clause were repealed, they said that the terms of admission to the Company were very easy, and that their regulations prevented everything of the nature of a monopoly. If the Italian merchants were acquainted with the proceedings which we have just detailed, they would know what value to attach to these assurances. There was indeed a large class who looked with disfavour on any measure calculated to strengthen the position of the Company against independent merchants. It was said that the Company did not attempt to prove to the Committee of the House the truth of any of the statements they had advanced in favour of the Bill. In the present case, there was no reason for repealing any part of the Navigation Act in favour of a Company already so far a monopoly as to enjoy unmolested the direct trade, which in peace was an advantage of 8 per cent., and in a French war, 20 per cent. over all others. The demand of the Company also conflicted with the interests of another influential body of men—the importers of drugs. By the Bill before the House, the importation from Italy of drugs of the growth of Asia would be prohibited. The Turkey merchants already had the advantage of importing these drugs direct from Asia, paying a duty of 35 per cent., while outsiders, who competed with them, had the heavy load of a 65 per cent. duty, "besides at least 20 per cent. more for freight and charges of passing through different hands from Turkey to Italy." Yet, they alleged, such was the inefficiency and ignorance of the Turkey merchants, that the kingdom was supplied from Italy in British shipping, woollen manufactures and fish being exchanged for the drugs by the private traders to Italy.

§ 12. *Opposition to the Company.*

It was evident at this time that the management of the Company's affairs was falling into the hands of the few active members in London, who sought to direct its policy, not only against the interests of the nation as a whole, but also against the less influential amongst their own members. Meanwhile, the resources of the outsiders were increasing, their energy was great, and they competed with the Company with some success, in spite of the advantages of the latter.

The monopoly enjoyed by the Company was rather a drag on the enterprise of others than a total prohibition. It drove the outsiders into the adoption of more costly methods than the normal condition of the trade would have rendered necessary if it had been free and open to all; but such was their energy and enterprise that they could undersell the Turkey merchants, whose advantages were more than counterbalanced by their inefficiency in making use of them. Thus the Company, which in its early years undoubtedly helped to foster a new and important commerce, became in its declining years the chief obstacle in the way of its further development. The case against the Levant Company was summed up in a pamphlet published in 1753 (*Reflections on the Expediency of Opening the Trade to Turkey*). The anonymous author pointed out the complete change in the circumstances of the foreign trade of this country since the formation of the Levant Company 150 years before. At that time we were the pioneers in a new trade; there were difficulties to cope with which made such an organization necessary, and even salutary. But since that time there had taken place a great extension of the trade and commerce of other nations who had joined in the trade, and were eager to take advantage of every circumstance which would help them in their competition with England. Now, the manner in which the Company organized their commerce seriously handicapped England in her struggle with other nations, especially France. Their practice of employing only the general ships of the Company led to inconvenience and expense. The charges for carriage to London, for factors, &c., were a heavy tax on the manufacturers, sufficient to turn the balance in favour of "our rivals the French, the natural enemies of our commerce." The expenses of package, porterage, and the custom-house fees were more exorbitant in London than in any other port of the United Kingdom, nor could the victualling of ships be accomplished so cheaply in London as in other ports. Thus the regulations of the Company enhanced prices, diminished the exportation of home commodities and the importation of foreign goods, such as raw silk, which were necessary for the development of English manufactures. If trade were free, the competition between individual merchants would lead to cheapness. But the chief competition in this struggle for the liberty of commerce was not between one English merchant and another, but between Great Britain and France. We had many advantages over the French in the Levant trade, if we chose to avail ourselves of them. English manufacturers could easily rival the French in Turkey cloth; and almost all other parts of a cargo to the Levant could be purchased more cheaply in England than at Marseilles, where also freight, insurance, and interest were higher. It was the Levant Company which blocked the progress of the trade. The continuation of the Company was, in effect, nothing else than the payment of a large tribute annually to France.

It was easy for the Company to reply to some of these objections, and to point out other causes than those alleged for the decay of the Levant trade. But in the main its opponents were right, and the time had come when its dissolution would be beneficial to the community. One difficulty in bringing this about was removed in 1803, when the Government assumed the appointment of the ambassadors and secretaries in Turkey. Twenty-two years later it was represented to the Company that their continued existence as a privileged corporation was no longer desirable. They quietly acquiesced in their extinction and surrendered their charter, after an existence of 260 years.

§ 13. *Early History of the East India Company.*

The East India Company may almost be considered an offshoot of the Levant Company. It will be remembered that the Muscovy merchants tried to open up a trade with Persia for raw silk, and in these expeditions came in contact with the traders of India and China. The Levant Company afterwards attempted an overland trade to India. They obtained East India goods at Agra, Bengal, and even at Malacca, and on the return brought information of the wealth which might be acquired by developing the trade. So the minds of English merchants were directed to the practicability of a direct communication by sea with the Indies. In 1589, they addressed a memorial to the Queen for permission to send ships to the Indies, and several voyages were undertaken, which were partly promoted by Turkey merchants. The success of the Dutch stimulated English efforts. East India commodities were the foundation of the trade of the Netherlands with the North of Europe. These they obtained from Lisbon, and Philip II. could scarcely have devised a better method of crippling their resources than prohibiting their trade with that port. Undaunted, however, by this measure, they sought for a direct route with India, and, after several fruitless attempts at a north-east passage, found their way round the Cape of Good Hope. Associations of merchants were formed, and they quickly established their trade. It is said that they raised the price of pepper against England; at any rate, their rapid progress hastened the formation of the London East India

Company. In 1599 a petition was presented to Elizabeth by a number of merchants who had subscribed £30,133 6*s.* 8*d.* in 100 shares, the subscriptions of individuals varying from £100 to £3000. They asked if they might be incorporated into a joint stock company, "for that the trade of the Indies being soe remote, could not be traded on but on a joint and united stock,"—that their shipping should not be stopped "as the delay of one month might lose a whole year's viage," for permission to export bullion, and for freedom from customs for six voyages. In granting this charter, Elizabeth had to guard against possible complications with Spain and the Netherlands, and against the complaints which her own subjects might bring of encroachments on their trade. The East India Company was incorporated on December 31st, 1600. The regulation of the trade and the sale of the merchandise were entrusted to a governor and twenty-four assistants, or "committees," as they were called, who were to be elected annually. At general assemblies laws might be made, so long as they were not contrary to the law of England, which they could enforce by fine and imprisonment. They might acquire lands, negotiate for trade privileges, appoint their factors and agents. A monopoly was granted to them of the trade to Asia, Africa, and all the islands, ports, etc., of Asia, Africa, and America, beyond the Cape of Good Hope to the Straits of Magellan. They were granted exemption from customs for the first four years. An important clause, which provoked much controversy, and the discussion of which greatly modified mercantilist views, gave them permission to export bullion. These privileges were limited to members of the Company, but they might grant licenses to others to trade with the Indies.

From the very first the English Company had to reckon with the rivalry of the Portuguese and the Dutch. The former had settled at Goa in 1497, and under the system of free enterprise which they practised, their trade increased during the sixteenth century. Their settlements were strong; but, after the usurpation of the Crown of Portugal by Philip II., who conferred a monopoly of the trade on a company of Spanish and Portuguese merchants, their strength became exhausted; fleets and reinforcements were no longer sent to resist the encroachments of the Dutch; and after a few years' fruitless struggle, they lost their superiority. But they were strong enough to give a good deal of trouble to their rivals, and numerous disputes occurred. The Dutch, however, were the chief opponents of the English Company. The different associations of merchants which were formed in Holland for trading to the East Indies were consolidated, in 1602, into one great company, and invested with the monopoly of the trade and various rights of sovereignty. Their constitution, however, was very different from that of the English companies which have been discussed. While the latter were constantly open to attack, on the ground that they confined the trade to a small section of the community, the Dutch Company derived much of its strength from its political position, and, in its early years at any rate, its peculiar constitution made the trade of almost "as general an advantage as if it were free and open." The capital of the Company was administered by a court of sixty-five directors, chosen by the different towns of the republic, each of which elected a number proportionate to its shares in the stock of the association; and the amount of these was determined by that of their respective contributions to the general taxes of the State.

"The constitution of the Company, therefore, was exactly analogous to that of the Commonwealth: it was virtually, even in its original formation, a department of Government in a country so essentially commercial." Thus the Dutch Company had a great advantage over their English rivals in any dispute which arose. While the former could bring to bear all the power and influence of the States-General, the latter could invoke the protection of the Government only by the ordinary method of petitioning the Sovereign. During the first twelve years of the English Company's existence, their operations consisted of little more than voyages of experiment. The Dutch, therefore, secured the temporary monopoly of the most valuable articles of Indian produce. They made large profits, and their prosperity was almost unbroken for sixty years. When they asked for a renewal of their charter in 1665, loud complaints were raised, which were supported by De Witt, on the ground that a free trade might be carried on at a far less expense, and would bring larger profits than an encumbered commerce. The States-General, however, renewed the Company's charter.

When the East India Company was founded, the majority of English merchants had by no means overcome the unwillingness to risk their capital in distant and uncertain undertakings, which thirty years before they had shown in the Levant trade; and for thirteen years the transactions of the Company consisted mainly of voyages of experiment, carried out at the expense of subordinate associations of stockholders. This extreme caution is the more remarkable when we consider the enormous profits, sometimes 230 per cent., which were made on these early voyages. In 1612 the directors decided to amalgamate these various associations, and that for the future the trade should be carried on by a joint stock only. The profits in this first undertaking by the Company in its corporate capacity are said to have amounted to 120 per cent. on the original subscription of £429,000, but they were subsequently diminished by the difficulties with the Dutch at the Spice Islands. The list of the subscribers in 1617 to the second joint stock of £1,629,000, shows how widespread the interest in the trade was becoming when once confidence was won. They included "15 dukes and earls, 13 countesses and other titled ladies, 82 knights (including judges and privy councillors), 18 widows and maiden-ladies, 26 clergymen and physicians, 313 merchants, 214 tradesmen, 25 merchant strangers, and 248 without any designation; total, 954."

§ 14. *The Amboyna Outrages.*

But the Company was now to enter upon a period of distress, which continued until after the Restoration. Some of the incidents of that period bring into strong relief the difficulties which the merchants of that time had to face, with the good and the evil of the methods adopted. The first is the dispute with the Dutch, at the Spice Islands. "More blood has been spilt over cloves," says Professor Thorold Rogers, "than over some dynasties. More unforgiven injuries have been committed in order to secure a monopoly of this spice than over anything except the monopoly of religious dogmas"—exaggerated language perhaps; yet, if we gave in detail the incidents which led to the rise in the price of cloves and other spices after 1622, we should have to speak of many a bitter struggle and some heroic acts of endurance. The English and Dutch at the Spice Islands were solving a problem which was at the root of the commercial wars of the eighteenth century, namely, in what circumstances was a peaceful trade possible with the newly-discovered countries; which, again, was only preliminary to the larger problem, still unsolved, of the subordination of local and national interests to the economic welfare of society as a whole. The history of the dispute has been told at length by Mr. Gardiner. The Dutch were directing all their efforts to the monopoly of the trade of the Spice Islands, from which they drove out the Portuguese. The English, coming later into the field, desired to prevent this, and, if they could not secure the monopoly for themselves, at any rate to get a share in so lucrative a commerce. The rival traders constantly came to blows, and there was no strong native authority to maintain an even balance between them. Negotiations were opened, broke down, and were renewed in 1619, when an attempted reconciliation of the rival claims was made. This treaty constituted a Council of Defence, consisting of an equal number of the representatives of both companies, for the management of the trade; fixed the proportions in which each should contribute to its defence; and assigned two-thirds of the spice trade of the Moluccas to the Dutch, and one-third to the English. James I. refused to fulfil his part in the bargain. Hostilities recommenced after a short cessation, and finally the English were driven from Amboyna and the adjacent islands (1623). Many of them were murdered, and, soon afterwards, the Dutch found means to drive the agents and servants of the English Company out of all the other Spice Islands, and to plunder their property found in their factories. The Dutch apparently had no qualms of conscience at this outrage. The charter of the Company was renewed, without any mention of the massacre, and they realized a dividend of 25 per cent. The English Company at the time in vain tried to vindicate their rights; but thirty years afterwards Cromwell remembered the outrage. He forced the Dutch, much against their inclinations, to consent to have their proceedings characterized in the Treaty of 1654 as the "murder" at Amboyna, and made them pay £85,000 compensation. Mr. Gardiner points out the real weakness of the Treaty of 1619. "It did not arise from the refusal of the King to thrust English garrisons upon Dutch territory,—the proximate cause of failure,—but in the success of the English merchants in establishing a treaty right to share in the commerce of islands which were under the territorial sovereignty of another nation." Before free trade relations could subsist between the rival nations, "there was needed the adoption of *cujus regio, ejus commercium*, analogous to the principle of *cujus regio, ejus religio*." The expulsion of the English from the Spice Islands combined with other causes to destroy public confidence in the Company, and their prosperity declined. From 1617—1632 their profits never exceeded 12½ per cent., and their stock frequently sold at 30, 35, and 40 per cent. discount. Some of the members wished to "break up the Company, and leave the trade," but they were afraid of publicly avowing their design. Their exportation of bullion alarmed the prejudices of the narrow-minded, while the risks and losses of the voyages undermined the credit of the Company. They complained of "a malignant, popular, and mutinous party, who had ever been clamorous and mutinous against the Government and committees," and who sought revenge in the ruin of the Company. There appeared upon inquiry to be three grounds of discontent—an opinion that the King was hostile to their interests, want of protection of their privileges, and the losses they had sustained. There was "so strong and constant a resolution to divide and dissolve the present stock, that all hope of reunion and upholding of the trade wholly depended upon the grace of his Majesty, who is only able to give the remedy." This conclusion sounds strange enough in modern ears; but in the seventeenth century, when the King could do much to make or mar their fortunes, his favour and protection were not to be despised. The Company, however, did not dissolve. On the contrary, they invited subscriptions to a third joint stock, and fitted out new ships, but apparently without success.

Their distress and the keen opposition to them gave rise to the memorial which they in 1628 presented to the King. This "Petition and Remonstrance," reprinted in 1641, is interesting because it was written by Thomas Mun. It was especially directed against those who objected to the exportation of bullion by the Company, and contained a clear statement of the principles, which were afterwards elaborated in *England's Treasure by Foreign Trade.* "If the trade was unprofitable, let it be suppressed; if not, let it be supported and countenanced by some public declaration." It was more profitable than less remote trades; East India commodities were cheaper than when they were brought from Turkey; if the trade were encouraged, the customs would increase. It was pointed out that the East India trade was a good counterpoise to the Dutch. "The safetie of the kingdom consists not onely in its owne strength and wealth, but also in . . . . the performance of those things which will weaken those who are or may become our enemies." Spain had been weakened by the competition of England and Holland, and

Spanish treasure dispersed by "the canker of war." "All nations, who have no mines of their owne, are inriched with gold and silver by one and the same meanes . . . . the ballance of their forraigne trades," which is the true rule of treasure. The Hollanders were become wealthy and strong by nothing else but trade, which increased treasure by re-exportation. "It is not the keeping of our money in the kingdome which makes a quicke and ample trade, but the necessity and use of our wares in forraigne countries, and our want of their commodities which causeth the vent and consumption on all sides." This petition was intended to answer the objections commonly urged against the East India Company, and to obtain further encouragement and protection.

§ 15. *The Pepper Loan.*

The next incident was no less disastrous to the Company than disgraceful to the King. It is interesting too, because it shows how well-grounded in the seventeenth century was the fear of associating the Government too closely with a trading corporation—a subject frequently discussed on the occasion of the establishment of the Bank of England. In 1640-1 the King forced the Company to sell to the Crown all their pepper in store—2310 bags, or 607,522 lbs., at 2*s.* 1*d.* per lb., *i. e.* for £63,283 11*s.* 1*d.* For this sum, four bonds of £14,000 each and one for £7,283, were given by the farmers of the customs and by Lord Cottington, to the Company, and one of these bonds were to be paid regularly every six months. The pepper was sold by the King to different merchants for ready money at 1*s.* 8*d.* per lb., or for £50,626 17*s.* 1*d.* By this shameful transaction, therefore, the King practically raised a loan of £50,000 at 18 per cent. Frequent attempts were made to get payment of tl bonds, but without success. For more than two years afte wards it appeared that the sum of £50,000 was still due them; and the Commissioners of the Treasury proposed th as his Majesty had several parks, which were of little u and great charge, some of them might be sold in fee-far reserving a small rent to the Crown. The Company severe felt this loss; and it is probable, as Bruce observes, that tl failure of their fourth joint stock was partly due to tl pepper loan.

§ 16. *The Interlopers.*

In the case of the Hull merchants and the Musco Company, we have seen how another body of merchan with a strong case in their favour, fared under the Compa organization. The East India Company was not allow to carry on its exclusive trade without interruption fro rival associations or other groups of merchants. As in t case of the other companies, the "interlopers" were important factor to be reckoned with.

The general character of State interference in the seve teenth century has been pointed out. Instead of upholdi the equal right of all citizens to share in the trade of t country, the Government became the tool of this or th section of the community, and pushed its interests to t exclusion of others. The private traders who were n fortunate enough to belong to one or other of the gre companies practically had no outlet for their energi They were looked upon with suspicion. They had rights—except that of keeping out of the way of others. the companies had been conducted on the principle whi was indicated at the beginning of this chapter, the private traders would have had no case. But they were absolutely excluded from the Joint Stock Companies by the fact that the stock, limited in amount, was in the hands of a few individuals, and the monopoly of the regulated companies was virtually as rigid. No one was excluded if he would pay the fees and submit to the regulations imposed by the Company. But these were frequently sufficient to take away all prospect of a reasonable profit. The interlopers, therefore, deserve some gratitude for their efforts to break through the exclusive privileges of the companies. The numerous cases which reached the law courts show that the East India Company suffered much from the depredations of private traders, who resorted to the Indies in defiance of their charter. But they had great difficulty in fighting so powerful a corporation. Even so late as 1684, when popular opinion against the Company was very strong, and their corrupt practices well-known, the case of Captain Thomas Sandys, who had fitted out a ship for the East India trade on his own account, was decided against him, and he had to sell ship and cargo at a great loss. There is evidence also of a clandestine trade carried on by the servants of the Company. So they needed all the protection they could get, if they intended to preserve their monopoly. There was another class of interlopers who could inflict great damage on the Company's interests—the traders or associations of traders who secured privileges from the king, in contravention of their charter. They suffered from the competition of these people almost from the formation of the Company, for James I., in 1604, granted a license to Sir Edward Michelborne and others to trade to "Cathaia, China, Japan, Corea, and Cambaya." The most important body was Courten's Association, or the "Assada Merchants," as they were called. In 1637 Charles I. granted a license to Sir William Courten and others to trade to Goa, Malabar, and China. Their first voyages were not successful, but their unwillingness in 1649-50 to amalgamate with the East India Company, on the recommendation of the Council of State, seems to indicate that they were well satisfied with their profits. A union, however, was finally agreed upon between the two associations, and some members of a third body—the "Merchant Adventurers trading to the Indies." It is said that the news of this united joint stock so greatly improved the Company's credit, that they could at any time borrow £20,000 at 12 per cent.! But these three bodies obviously would not work in harmony with each other, for each desired the monopoly of the trade. So the "interlopers" got up an agitation for an open trade. A pamphlet, *Strange News from India*, was published in 1652. The author complained that the Company was a destructive monopoly, that "our people in the beginning of the East India trade had made particular running voyages thither, only, to enrich a few, they were afterward united in a joint stock company." This pamphlet was written in the interest of Courten's heirs, and so its statements should be received *cum grano salis.* In 1654 the interlopers petitioned Cromwell for an open trade, and the question was referred to a Select Committee. During the negotiations it is said that the Company's trade was more or less suspended at Surat, in Persia, and Bantam, and that they suffered heavy losses from the Dutch, and by the desertion of their servants. Private traders seized the opportunity to rush into the trade, and great disorganization prevailed. The available evidence appears on the whole to bear out the

Company's assertion that the open trade of these three years resulted in an enhancement of prices.

There is a curious incident which shows in what manner the new conditions of trade were expected to affect the value of the official posts in India. Richard Wild begged Thurloe to use his influence with the Protector to secure for him the consulship at Surat. If he would do so, Wild promised to pay him £500 per annum as long as he held the consulship, in addition to a share of the pearl fishing formerly agreed upon. Thurloe, on his part, was to prevail with the Protector to grant him the consulship for three years or more, with an allowance of 2 per cent. as in the case of other consuls in Turkey and elsewhere, or 2½ per cent. "in regard of the long and tedious voyage thither, and the custom of those countries to give great presents to the governors and chief men every year, besides all other occasions, which happen extraordinary; all which must be defrayed out of the consul's allowance." Besides the payment to Thurloe himself, Wild promised "unto Mr. Secretaire's ladie one fair jewell, sett with eighteen fassett diamonds and three pendant diamonds." If the Protector renewed the Company's charter, he asked Thurloe to recommend him to be their President at Surat. But in this case the above-mentioned £500 a year was "to be laid aside and void. The jewell only shal be presented as before, with such other rarities out of India as shall manifest the said Richard Wylde's thankfulness for Mr. Secretarie's favour and assistance herein." In 1656-7 Cromwell decided that the only remedy for the disorganized condition of the trade was the renewal of the Company's charter.

The severe treatment which Thomas Skinner, one of the merchants who had taken advantage of the "open trade" to engage in a voyage to the East Indies and to establish a warehouse at Jamba, received at the hands of the newly-chartered Company, gave rise to the famous conflict with regard to the jurisdiction of the House of Lords, in the case *Skinner* v. *The East India Company* (1666).

§ 17. *Character of the Opposition to the East India Company.*

We can now understand the opposition to the East India Company, which found expression in many pamphlets, contending for a free and open trade. These writers did not desire free trade in the modern sense of the words; for the most part they did not desire the dissolution of the trading companies. They wished to see the joint stock superseded by the regulated companies, and admission to the latter made as easy as possible. They hated the private trader as much as any monopolist. To the seventeenth century merchant the unfettered competition of one with another meant chaos. An unregulated trade "opened a gap and let in all sorts of unskilful and disorderly persons." The true course was a *via media* between strict monopoly and free competition. A free trade, regulated, was favourable to individual enterprise, developed mercantile talent, and cheapened foreign commodities. During the seventeenth century the controversy was perpetually recurring, on the respective merits of the two methods of carrying on trade; on the occasion of the Free Trade Bills in 1604, the disputes of the Hull merchants with the Muscovy Company, the struggle of the interlopers in the East Indies, the case of the Levant Company, and the resistance to the African Company in 1695, and at other times.

It is easy to understand the opposition of the Levant to

the East India Company, for the direct sea route to India first ruined their spice trade, and then crippled their trade in raw silk. Hence they were continually agitating for the withdrawal of the East India Company's charter, and the formation of a new association similar to their own. Child and other writers maintained that experience was in favour of the joint stock system for the East India trade. No other nation except the Portuguese had traded otherwise. They pointed to the costly presents which it was necessary to make to the native princes; the charges and hazards in the maintenance of their privileges; the securities for factors, cost of warehouses, and forts; and the difficulty of getting redress for private traders. It was also maintained that the joint stock system was far more national with respect to the number of persons benefited than a regulated company could be. For, while only skilled merchants and wealthy people who could afford to "lie at least two years out of their money," could avail themselves of the latter, the former gave facilities for investment to countless people whose savings otherwise would not assist in the development of trade.

The Company had the best of the argument on the advantages of the joint stock principle. What they did not see was the evil result of conferring upon them a monopoly of the trade, a course which threw the control of the trade into the hands of a very small minority of the nation. It appeared, in the proceedings before the Privy Council in 1681, that there were only 600 persons on the Company's books—a considerable fall from 954 in 1617, and that some of the stockholders had as many as sixty votes. When we have said that the East India Company produced some sound arguments in favour of the joint stock principle we have said all we can for them at the end of the seventeenth century. Their enemies accused them of securing a continuance of their charter by bribing Charles II. and James II. They admitted the payment of 10,000 guineas into the Exchequer, for the public services! And it appeared in the Parliamentary inquiry in 1695 that great sums had been expended for special services, of which no explanation could be given. *Houghton's Price Lists of East India Stock*, printed by Professor Thorold Rogers, are eloquent on the condition of the old East India Company in its last years, and the stormy agitation of that time.

§ 18. *The New East India Company.*

In 1692 the Commons addressed King William to dissolve the old and incorporate a new company. It was found that the Company could not be dissolved without three years' notice being given, so the address was renewed the following year with this modification. The interest in the subject was great, and as it became evident that the charter of the Company was in danger, their stock steadily fell. On March 30th, 1692, it was at 158; by the middle of June it had fallen to 137. The average for the next year, in which they managed by bribes to gain a renewal of their charter, was only 92, their stock falling from 146 on February 10th to 92 before the end of the year. In the year of the Parliamentary inquiry alluded to above (1695), it continued to fall, with fluctuations of as much as from 93 on September 6th to 77 on September 13th. In 1698, a number of merchants, anxious to break down the Company's monopoly, offered £2,000,000 at 8 per cent. to the Government, on condition of having conferred upon them the privileges of the Indian trade. In consequence of this offer, a loan from the old Company of £700,000 at 4 per cent. was rejected. It is said that so great was the expectation of advantages from a company trading under Parliamentary authority, that the whole £2,000,000 was subscribed in three days after the books were opened, of which £315,000 came from the old Company. The charter of the old Company had still three years to run; nevertheless a new company was erected in September 1698, when old East India Stock was at 41, and the two continued together. By an omission in their charter some of the members of the new Company were able to separate their concerns from the general joint stock. There were thus four classes of merchants trading to the East Indies at this time—(1) the old East India Company, who were to continue for three years, and who had subscribed £315,000 to the new Company, doubtless with the idea of obtaining some control in its affairs; (2) the new English East India Company, who, though unprovided with forts and factories, were authorized to trade to the full extent of their capital; (3) the members of the new Company who refused to unite in the joint stock, and who, with their capital of £7200, were a kind of third company; and (4) the separate traders who had despatched their ships before July 1st, 1698, and had the right to continue their voyage for one year. The presence of these rival traders produced a state of confusion and depression, in 1699, unparalleled in the history of the Companies. In the following year, however, there was some improvement. The old Company's stock rose pretty steadily, though the average for the whole year (112) was considerably below that of the new Company, which was 145. In 1701, the stock of both Companies again fell, the average being

83 and 112 respectively. At length, in 1702, the old and new companies consented to preliminary terms of agreement, when the price of stock rose to 105 and 136. Four years later they were incorporated under the title of the United Company of Merchants of England trading to the East Indies. This course—reform not destruction of the old system, the creation of an English East India Company under Parliamentary sanction—was, on the whole, the right one. Certainly, having regard to the years of agitation, it is difficult to see what other course could have been pursued with advantage, if the trade was to be fostered. The old Company grew out of associations formed with the Royal sanction for merely commercial purposes. In the peculiar relation of the Government to the Company, it was inevitable that the latter should be forced by the difficulties of the trade to assume territorial rights of sovereignty. This tendency, which might have been discerned early in its history, became more marked under the new conditions. We cannot here trace its subsequent development; but looking back over the history of the last 300 years, the formation of the new East India Company, under Parliamentary sanction, falls into its place as the most important step of the seventeenth century, in the creation of the British Empire in the East.

§ 19. *The Conclusion.*

It may be justly doubted if there was ever any economical justification for the existence of the Trading Companies. Their organization was rendered necessary by the political conditions under which the foreign trade of the country had to be developed. Those conditions were unfavourable to economic progress, for, although in a time of general insecurity and want of confidence, an individual or a nation may be stimulated to greater exertions, and may snatch certain advantages at the expense of others, trade can only flourish in peace, reverence for the law, security to person and property, mutual confidence and integrity in commercial dealings. The Trading Companies continued to exist when there was no longer any necessity for them. If the political duties they were able to fulfil fostered the trade of the country, the influence which the increase of their wealth gave them in Parliament helped to continue their monopoly and blocked the way to reform. The history of the Trading Companies is not without its warnings at a time when certain powerful "interests" have undue influence in the English representation. Nor is the history of that time favourable to a close association of the Government with trade. State interference with trade has generally meant class legislation, and favour shown to one section of the community at the expense of others. This must be so when one class is the dominating power in the State. In the seventeenth century we can at any rate see the opinion gaining ground that no power but that of Parliament had the right to interfere with the trade of English subjects. The reform of the East India Company, and the curtailment of the privileges of the other companies, are its formal expression.

CHAPTER IV.

THE WORKING CLASSES: CRAFTSMEN AND LABOURERS.

§ 1. *The Statute of Apprenticeship.*

THERE is no reason for supposing that the policy of confiscation pursued by Henry VIII. and his successors brought that ruin on the craftsmen which has been placed amongst the principal causes of poverty in the sixteenth and the seventeenth centuries. It was pointed out by the London Livery Companies' Commission (1884) that the Statute of 1547 extended only to the gild lands which were held to "superstitious uses."[1] All other lands of the mysteries and crafts were exempted from the operation of the Act. The London Companies were allowed to redeem their confiscated lands on the ground that they were required for the support of the charities of which they were the trustees. The Merchant Taylors of Bristol were allowed the same privilege. It is probable that the surviving members of the trading gilds and corporations divided the remaining property amongst themselves as those institutions died out. Their powers were untouched by the Statute of Monopolies (1624), which did not extend to companies and mysteries of crafts; and it is evident from contemporary records that they continued

[1] Cf. Cunningham, *Growth of English Industry and Commerce*, p. 465.

throughout the seventeenth century, and, in some instances, far into the eighteenth, to control the industries of the towns where they were established. The researches of Dr. Gross, whose admirable work on the gild merchant throws more light on the history and constitution of the gilds than any book ever published, enable us to see the transformation which actually took place. The growth of the craft gilds split up the functions of the ancient gild merchant, which were undertaken by the new associations. Along with this movement, which can be traced during the fourteenth and the fifteenth centuries, when the craft gilds were at the height of their prosperity and influence, the growth of a more intimate connection between the gilds and the municipality can be discerned as trade and industry increased. Freedom to exercise a trade and the civic franchise became interdependent, "the one being a necessary condition for the attainment of the other, or constituting a legitimate claim to it." Freedom to exercise a trade was obtained generally by apprenticeship; and, keeping this in mind, it is evident that the re-integration during the sixteenth and seventeenth centuries of the various parts into which the functions of the gild merchant had been separated, and the closer bond between the reorganized crafts and the municipality, enabled the boroughs to maintain a monopoly, and threw upon them important duties in the regulation of trade. The reorganization of the crafts took various forms, but the most usual was their division into companies, to carry into effect regulations which applied to all trades alike. The most important of their functions was the enforcement of apprenticeship as a condition for the exercise of trade or handicraft. This was the state of things in towns where the gild organization survived.

But there is evidence of the birth of new trades, or the development of old ones, which were outside the influence of such an organization; and there must have existed for a long time bodies of artisans who felt none of the hardships if they shared none of the privileges of the old gilds. There were also towns and districts where no gild existed, subject only in their trade and industry to the law of the land.

It was in these circumstances that the famous Statute of Apprenticeship was passed (Stat. 5 Eliz. c. 4, 1562). The preamble points out the failure of former statutes, "partly through the imperfection and contrariety" in the laws themselves, and "chiefly for that the wages and allowances .... are too small, and not answerable to this time respecting the advancement of prices of all things." The Legislature proposed, therefore, "to digest and reduce into one sole law" the substance of the old statutes, in the hope that the new law (duly executed) would "banish idleness, encourage husbandry, and yield unto the hired person, both in time of scarcity and in the time of plenty, a convenient proportion of wages." Former statutes, thirty-nine in number since Edward III., were repealed so far as they concerned the hiring, keeping, wages, etc., of servants, labourers, artificers, and apprentices. Single persons under thirty years of age, having neither lands nor tenements to the yearly value of 40*s.*, nor goods of the value of £10, were compelled to serve in the crafts to which they had been brought up; and all persons not otherwise employed, nor possessing a certain amount of property, were compelled to serve in husbandry. The latter clause was supplemented with a law of settlement, which, however, was relaxed in time of harvest. The apprenticeship clauses imposed certain property qualifications in all trades except those of smiths, wheelwrights, plasterers, bricklayers, and a few other crafts. The term of apprenticeship was seven years, with a penalty of 40*s.* a month for any time short of that period. Every person with three apprentices must keep one journeyman, and for every other apprentice another journeyman. Penalties of imprisonment were imposed on those who refused to be apprenticed, and the limit of age at which indentures might be signed was twenty-one. The Act was administered by the Justices of the Peace, or other magistrates specified. They were empowered to fix the rate of wages in their districts, at the Easter Quarter Sessions, and to enforce this rate by fine and imprisonment. They were also to arbitrate in disputes between masters and apprentices. The hours of labour were to be from 5 a.m. till 6 or 8 p.m. in the summer, and from daylight to dusk in the winter, not more than two and a half hours being allowed for meals. By 39 Eliz. c. 12, the Act was extended to weavers. It was continued by 43 Eliz. c. 9, and 1 Jac. I. c. 6, the latter of which empowered the justices and town magistrates to fix limits to the wages of all labourers and workmen whatever. The statute was supplemented by several laws passed in the reigns of Charles II. and William III.

It was not intended that this statute should supersede the organization of the crafts in the boroughs. On the contrary, that organization would supply the best machinery for enforcing its provisions relating to apprenticeship. The crafts would perform much the same function as a modern trade union in the administration of the Factory Acts. They would constitute a kind of "vigilance association," and it would be in the towns and districts where no such organization existed that the greatest difficulty would be felt in enforcing the statute. It is important to decide what was the effect of this piece of legislation, for great influence has been ascribed to it in the subsequent history of the working-classes. We have, on the one hand, those who see in it the success of a long and deliberate conspiracy of one class against another; while, on the other hand, there are those who regard it as the Great Charter of the working-classes, the means of resisting oppression and of obtaining fair conditions of employment, which the industrial revolution swept away. The following considerations may help to throw light on the actual working of the statute, and to place the period during which it was operative in its right relation to subsequent industrial history.

§ 2. *Apprenticeship.*

The difficulty of enforcing apprenticeship accelerated that change in the gild organization which took place in the sixteenth and seventeenth centuries, namely, the consolidation of the crafts for the regulation of trade, and a closer connection between them and the municipal authorities. The freemen jealously guarded their monopoly of the trade of the towns. Those who were detected in practising a trade without having served apprenticeship were punished in accordance with the law, and efforts were made to secure the enrolment of indentures. For example, on March 9th, 1578-9, the Common Council of Nottingham resolved that "all manner of apprentices already bound and to be bound should bring their indentures to be enrolled before May Day next, or else every Master to forfeit 12*d.* And the Mayor to admit no Burgess but by consent of the Wardens of the occupation they been of, or other two of the honestest of the occupation in default of the Wardens; and to have a special regard that such have been and served as apprentices and been enabled, according to the Statute of Anno 5 of Elizabeth." In the December before, an action was brought against one Thomas Nix for practising the trade of ironmonger, to which he had not been apprenticed, contrary to the statute. Many such cases are recorded in Middlesex, Devonshire, and Derbyshire. Sometimes towns obtained the privilege of organizing the freemen into companies, and the principal object they had in view was the maintenance of their monopoly; but the objections of the clothiers of Leeds, on the incorporation of that town in 1636, show that the craftsmen were not unanimously in favour of this course. At an assembly of the Mayor, Sheriffs, Aldermen, and Common Council of Norwich on August 19th, 1622, the companies of "divers trades and occupations" complained "that of late, for want of the perfection of those ancient established ordinances, and due execution of the same, many Forreners had bin admitted to the freedome of the City, without consent of the Headman and Wardens of any company or society of any trade or occupation, And that many, under pretence of Apprenticehood, had indevoured to obtaine the freedome, liberties and privileges of the Citty, where in truth they never served as Apprentices by the space of seven yeeres, according to the Lawes and Statutes of this Realme, and the Customes of the City of Norwich; and that many persons having taken Apprentices, had forborne to inroll their Indentures according to the Ordinances prescribed in that behalfe, whereby many Apprentices, after their tearme expired, had beene much troubled in procuring proofe of their service, and meanes to obtaine their freedome, and many other by fraudulent practices had unduly indevoured the obtaining thereof." An ordinance was then enacted to meet these evils "by the Mayor, Sheriffs, and Aldermen of the City, with the consent of the Common Council, upon the humble complaint and petition of many of the men of trades and occupations, with the consent of the greater number of them." Amongst the measures adopted was the division of the seventy-nine trades of the City into twelve grand companies, of which the Aldermen of the various wards were Masters. Then follow rules with regard to apprenticeship, the enrolment of indentures, searching for defective wares, etc. Not more than four were to be admitted, in any trade, to the freedom of the City in one year.

In the towns, therefore, some organization of the trades was necessary to guard the monopoly which was theoretically secured to the freemen by the law of the land; and so far as the efforts made to enforce apprenticeship were successful, competition was restrained within narrow limits. But where the gild organization was allowed to decay, or in the places where it had never existed, it would not be easy to enforce the law. Its due administration would depend solely on the loyal co-operation of those whom it concerned. If, on the one hand, the well-to-do craftsmen had every inducement to maintain the system of seven years' apprenticeship; there were, on the other hand, many poorer artisans to whom the law was a great hardship, and who would have to choose between fraudulent practices and no employment. Under the old Poor Law, only a moral genius would hesitate. That many persons did not consider it their interest to duly qualify themselves, is evident from the numerous cases of infringement of the statute. We have no means of determining the proportion of undetected offenders.

The attempts also to supplement the law with special

legislation for particular classes of workers indicate some difficulty in enforcing apprenticeship. In 1601 we find a Bill introduced into the House of Commons on behalf of the Company of Painters, "which had been time out of mind an ancient company within the City of London, and had lately been incorporated by letters patent, under which none but those duly apprenticed might practice the art or mystery of painting or painter-staining; but of late the plasterers had begun to infringe this law to the injury of duly apprenticed and skilled painters, and the increase of bad work." The Bill reached its second reading in the Lords, when counsel was ordered to be heard for both painters and plasterers, and the matters in dispute were referred to the Lord Mayor and Judges to decide. In 1624 a Bill was introduced for the "relief of the artisan cloth-workers of the City of London," by regulating the number of apprentices and journeymen to be employed by each master, and the rate of wages. The Civil Wars also gave rise to some infringements of the Statute of Apprenticeship. Twice, indeed, it was suspended. In 1642, apprentices who "listed to serve as soldiers for the defence of the kingdom," were absolved from fulfilling their indentures. Their masters were "to receive them again at the end of their service without imputing any loss of time to them, but the same should be reckoned as well spent, according to their indentures, as if they had been still in their shops." Again, in 1654, Stat. 5 Eliz., and all laws of corporations to the same effect, were suspended in favour of soldiers who had served the Commonwealth, and they were enabled to exercise any trade. Pardons, also, were sometimes granted to persons practising trades without having served apprenticeship. On the whole, therefore, apprenticeship even in the protected trades was not universally and strictly enforced during the seventeenth century.

§ 3. *The Regulation of Wages.*

The apprenticeship laws, however, must be studied in connection with the part of Stat. 5 Eliz. relating to wages, in order to judge of their full effect. It will be remembered that the statute empowered the Justices of the Peace, or other town magistrates specified in the Act, to fix wages, at the Easter Quarter Sessions. This was not so much a new departure as an extension of the powers of the Justices, who had before been entrusted with a wide jurisdiction in the regulation of wages. The object of the Act of 1562 appears to have been the adjustment of wages at shorter intervals of time and more in accordance with local variations in the price of provisions. Twenty-three assessments are known, of which Professor Thorold Rogers criticized twelve—Rutland (1562, 1610); Colchester (1583); Essex (1651, 1661); Chester (1591, 1594); York (1593); Devonshire (1594, 1654, 1714); Lancaster (1595); Lincolnshire (1619, 1621); Gloucester (1632, 1655, 1727); Derbyshire (1634, 1648); London (1655); Suffolk (1682); Warwickshire (1684); Bucks (1688). Thorold Rogers also alludes to a Lancashire assessment of 1725, and we know that assessments were made for Middlesex immediately after passing the statute, for, on June 20th, there is a case of a miller who gave excessive wages contrary to its provisions; and, on April 7th, 1609, the Justices decided that "the rates for servants' wages for this year should continue as before." We are, therefore, in possession of a large amount of evidence of the condition of the working-classes during 165 years, and there is no doubt that similar assessments were put forth for other parts of the country, from time to time.

Can we assume that, on the whole, the rate of wages sanctioned by the Justices was actually paid in the districts to which their decisions applied? A brief examination will show that with some qualification we may do so. Thorold Rogers' averages, for this period, show a *higher* rate of wages than was sanctioned in the assessments which he reviewed. But they are based on information derived mainly from Cambridge, Oxford, Eton, and Winchester; and, for the last thirty years of the seventeenth century, from London. There are few northern entries and this deficiency is specially marked in the building trades and in agricultural labour, to which the bulk of Thorold Rogers' information relates. Now, it is well known that wages and prices were at a lower level in the north of England than in the midland and southern counties. Yet, no northern rates enter into the averages with which he criticized the northern assessments. We should, therefore, expect some divergence tending to show that "the employers were more merciful than the Quarter Sessions," or, in other words, that the labourers were able to secure a higher rate of wages than was sanctioned by the Justices. We know that the Rutland rates (1610) were followed from 1626 to 1634. In the midlands and in the south-eastern counties there is no great difference between the Justices' rates and Professor Rogers' average rates. The Justices of Derbyshire (1648) and Essex (1651—1661) sanctioned rates in some instances higher than the averages. Local information on the whole confirms the Justices' assessments. London, of course, stands alone in the high wages paid to artisans.

In 1655, the Lord Mayor and the Justices issued the following assessment—

	s.	d.	
Carpenters, Bricklayers, Masons, &c., and other handicraftsmen	2	6	*per diem.*
Journeymen, or apprentice of two years' service...	2	0	,,
Labourers, and all other persons	1	0	,,

These were maximum rates. Turning now to Thorold Rogers' averages, we find that the rates in the same year are—for carpenters, 1*s.* 6*d.*; masons, 1*s.* 8*d.*; bricklayers, 1*s.* 8*d.*; carpenter and man, 2*s.* 6*d.*; mason and man, 3*s.* 2*d.*; joiner, 1*s.* 6*d.*; bricklayer and man, 2*s.* 8*d.*; and "labourer to artisan," 1*s.* These rates are considerably lower than the London assessment. The information on which they were based comes from Cambridge, Oxford, Basingstoke, Horstead Keynes (Sussex), and Winchester. The London rates again after 1671, show little or no advance on the assessment for 1655, quoted above, while in some instances there is a positive falling off. Possibly they followed an assessment which has not been preserved, for after the Great Fire, the Act for rebuilding the City of London enabled the Justices of the King's Bench to fix wages, "to the intent that no brickmaker, carpenter, etc., or other artificer, workman, or labourer may make the common calamity a pretence to extort unreasonable or excessive wages by combination or otherwise" (19 Car. II. c. 3).

The evidence of the Courts also is very instructive. Out of upwards of one hundred offences against the Labour Laws during the latter part of the sixteenth and the first half of the seventeenth centuries, there were only two cases of the payment of higher than the statutory wages. One of these was in 1561, before the Statute of Apprenticeship was passed; and the other in June, 1563, against a miller, under the assessment "recently made." The majority of the offences fall under the apprenticeship clauses. Now, on the whole, one would not expect the latter to occur *more* frequently than the payment of excessive wages, if the labourers could secure them, allowing even for greater difficulty or negligence in the detection of offenders. These facts confirm the impression that, generally speaking, the Justices' rates were actually paid.

It is difficult to say in what manner the Justices used the power which the Government placed in their hands, or whether they really tried to enforce their awards. In 1601, the Devonshire constables were ordered to ascertain the names of all masters and servants that gave or received higher wages than those appointed, and to report them to the Justices; and five sub-committees were appointed especially to attend to this matter in the different districts. This attempt to devise an efficient administrative system took place seven years after the rate of wages had been settled, which it was meant to carry into effect—a rate which was not altered during the reign of Elizabeth. This was the manner in which they administered an Act intended "to yield unto the hired person, both in time of scarcity and in the time of plenty, a convenient proportion of wages." How terrible must have been the hardships inflicted on the wage-earners, will be evident from the table on the following page. The first column in each case represents the Barnstaple prices, the second Thorold Rogers' averages for the same time.

An assessment was made for Bucks in 1688. Twelve years afterwards the Court considered "that the wages of artificers and labourers, as settled at the sessions, had not

Anno Domini.	Wheat.		Rye.		Barley.		Oats.	
	s. d.	*s. d.*	*s. d.*	*s. d.*	*s. d.*	*s. d.*	*s. d.*	*s. d.*
1586	64 0	45 8¾	40 0	31 0	42 8	14 0	—	—
August	80 0		21 4		18 0		—	—
1587 At Xmas.	21 4	16 0½	—	—	16 6	10 6¾	12 0	7 2¾
1588	21 4	15 0¼	—	—	13 4	10 4¾	7 4	7 7
before the	35 4	—	12 0	10 0	12 0	—	—	—
end.	24 0	26 11½	—	—	—	—	—	—
1590	53 4	25 4	—	—	—	—	—	—
1591	[1] —	18 1¼	—	—	—	—	—	—
1594	40 0	24 8¾	24 0	—	24 0	16 0	12 0	11 3
1595	72 0	37 7½	—	52 9½	—	—	—	—
	80 0		60 0	—	48 0	—	18 8	18 0¼
1596	96 0	40 9½	—	—	64 0	—	—	—
	120 0		—	36 0	100 0	—	29 4	—
Standard	72 0	56 6¼	48 0		40 0	25 5¼	40 0	14 1¾
1597	144 0		112 0	—	104 0		38 8	
In July	160 0	—	—	22 0	120 0	—	—	—
1598	64 0	52 4½	48 0		48 0	17 8½	14 8	9 11¼
	32 0				20 0		—	—
1599	26 8	31 1½	21 8	29 4	18 8	19 0	—	—
1601	42 8	34 9	34 8	28 9½	29 4	18 5½	—	—
1602	69 4	24 2	50 8	18 8	40 0	19 0	14 8	8 0¼
1604	53 4	26 7¼	40 0	—	29 4	15 0	—	—

for many years been altered, notwithstanding that by the consent of masters and servants the same had been generally increased both in the Vale and the Chiltern, whereby both masters and servants had been and were subjected to indictments for their disobedience and contempts of the orders of the Court." They decided to reconsider the rate of wages at the next session, but they took no further measures. The Orders for the relief of the Poor (1630) directed Justices of the Peace to see that the statute "be not deluded by private contracts;" and if we may accept the statements in contemporary pamphlets, many Justices were not over

[1] Provisions very dear.

zealous in the administration of the law. There was probably no need for them to enforce their awards at a time when wages were effectually reduced by the ordinary method of competition. They were the last people in the world who should have been entrusted with an operation of such difficulty and complexity as the regulation of wages. They endeavoured to do so only at long intervals of time, when they probably talked matters over with the employers in the district, and gave a legal sanction to the current rate of wages, which they took as the maximum. Thus the statute would become an instrument of oppression in the hands of unscrupulous employers. They could effectually crush all attempts to secure an advance, if they cared to do so, by legal proceedings against delinquents, in which they would certainly be supported by the Justices. We may well believe that many employers, themselves ground down by the landlords, or subjected to keen competition in the towns, would use the Wages Assessments as an excuse for harshly treating the labourers, when they could find no other justification. On the whole, therefore, we may accept the Justices' rates as representing current wages in the various counties at the time they were put forth. When we have two or three assessments for the same county, we may assume that wages have only fluctuated slightly during the intervals between the limits indicated. It is, for example, very improbable that the Devonshire Justices in 1654 would have deliberately *returned* to a rate little above that of 1594, if during the interval there had been any considerable increase. The assessments, therefore, render valuable aid in the interpretation of Thorold Rogers' averages, and combining the two sources of information, we can take a fairly comprehensive survey of the condition of the labourers.

§ 4. *Real Wages in the Seventeenth Century.*

Making Thorold Rogers' statistics the basis of our calculations, let us see what was the condition of the average labourer from 1583 to 1702. It is best to divide the 120 years into three periods of forty years each. In the first, money wages fluctuated between 5*s*. $\frac{3}{8}$*d*. and 5*s*. 8$\frac{1}{4}$*d*. per week, and show, on the whole, a very slow rate of increase.[1] In the second period there was a fairly steady and much more rapid improvement; and, in the last, the labourers did little more than maintain the position they had secured. The highest weekly rate for the whole period was 9*s*. If the rate of increase during the first forty years be represented by unity, then the rates for the second and third periods was about 5·0513 and ·437. The rate of improvement for the 120 years was about $\frac{1}{175}$. The condition of the labourer, however, is seen much more clearly if we find out how far their wages would go in purchasing the necessaries of life. For this purpose, it is sufficient, for a rough comparison of one year with another, to adopt a uniform standard of comfort, and to calculate the degree in which the average labourer approached or receded from it. If we wished to be very exact, we should of course be compelled to adopt a much more elaborate method. It is convenient to adopt the standard suggested by Thorold Rogers, namely, two quarters of wheat, two quarters of malt, one quarter of oatmeal, and a fixed allowance for rent, clothes, tools, etc., for a labourer, his wife, and four children, for one

[1] "Rate of increase" and "rate of improvement" means here and throughout the chapter what Professor Marshall calls the *average proportionate rate of increase*, i. e. the fraction of the wages which must be added year by year from 1583 to obtain those of 1622, etc.

year. This is a moderate allowance. It is then found that, from 1583 to 1622, the mean proportion of this standard which the average artisan could annually purchase was 73 per cent.; in the second period, from 82 to 84 per cent.; and in the third period, from 98 to 100 per cent. From 1583 to 1622, however, the standard of comfort *declined*, and the average artisan must have resorted to a standard inferior even to that which prevailed from 1541 to 1583; while in some years he starved. During the second period there was a very marked improvement; the rate of increase being nearly double that of the third period (1663—1702). But, taking the whole period (1583—1702), the rise in the standard of comfort was less rapid than the rise in wages. This paragraph may be summed up with the remark that, from 1583 to 1622, the wages of the average artisan were considerably below subsistence, on the standard adopted; from 1623 to 1662, they were lifted to the level of subsistence at the same standard; and from 1663 to 1702 they effected a slight improvement on the condition then attained.

§ 5. *Qualifications to the Foregoing Statement.*

This statement of the condition of the working-classes in the seventeenth century is subject to some qualifications. The first and most obvious one is that this condition was not uniform over the whole country. Strictly speaking, Thorold Rogers' averages can be accepted only for the W., S., S.E., and E. counties. Other districts do not show so low a degree of adversity as these figures indicate. Unfortunately, we have not sufficient information of wages and prices in the north of England to reduce the condition of the labourers to exact numerical measurement. It is very desirable that all local records should be published or made as accessible as possible. But, if the assessments are a safe guide, and for the reasons given we may on the whole so consider them, and using the scattered data which we have, it is not far from the truth to say that money wages were 50 per cent. lower than the above rates, and the standard of comfort from 35 to 40 per cent. lower. In this statement are included the counties north of a line drawn from the Dee to the Wash, and south of the northern boundary of Lancashire and Yorkshire. About the counties farther north we have not sufficient information to venture on a general statement. Lincolnshire seems to have been better than the other northern counties, but behind Derbyshire, which shows some improvement between 1634 and 1648. The lead miners, however, were very badly off; and some of the Derbyshire Justices won for themselves a reputation for harshness and oppression. The Black Country, where there was considerable industrial activity, Salop, Worcester, and Hereford were on a higher level than the north but lower than the E., W., and S.E. The worst county of all appears to have been Warwickshire, where, in 1684, the rates were little better than the northern rates a century before. Bucks is better than Warwick only in the skilled trades. Agriculture shows little advance on the northern rates, and no advance on the Devonshire rates of the reign of Elizabeth. Devonshire money wages start on the same level as Thorold Rogers' averages, but show no advance for sixty years. This county does not appear to have shared in the upward movement during the Protectorate, and from 1654 to 1714, the increase is very small. Prices also were double the average. In spite of the development of the woollen trade, it is difficult to resist the conclusion that the rate of improvement in Devonshire was slower than in the rest of the country.

§ 6. *Irregularity of Employment.*

We come now to the second qualification to the above statement of the average condition of the working-classes. That is the allowance which must be made for *irregularity of employment.* In dealing with the purchasing power of wages we assumed a working year of three hundred days, or of fifty weeks of six days each. It is convenient to do this for various reasons. Most students of economic history read Thorold Rogers' *Work and Wages*, and in this book and the larger one on which it is founded, the same assumption is made. If, therefore, we now keep to it, we shall be able to bring these scattered remarks into clearer relation with a work which for many years must remain the principal source of information about labour and wages in the past, and which, in its most valuable characteristics, can never be superseded. But this is not a sufficient reason for working on an erroneous hypothesis. It will be remembered, however, that the standard adopted was for a man, his wife and family of four children. Now, in making the calculations, the earnings of all except the head of the family have been neglected, and these might sometimes have been considerable. We have also neglected a possible alternative occupation or occupations which the wage-earner could occasionally take up when his main source of livelihood temporarily failed him, and the help the family obtained by the cultivation of a little land or a garden. Unfortunately we have not sufficient information to measure these sources of income. But, on the whole, we may assume that the earnings of the normal family, in these various ways, would be equivalent to the earnings of an adult male employed at the current rate of wages continuously for 300 days in the year.

The *fact* of the irregularity of employment during the seventeenth century is clear. Complaints of the "unemployed," appeals to the Legislature to remedy the evil, schemes for finding work for such people, riots in various parts of the country when the poorer craftsmen clamoured for food or work, petitions, and the administration of the Poor Law, supply plenty of evidence of the constant recurrence of periods of depression throughout the century. The Government tried to meet the evil with special measures for the encouragement of different trades, and by compelling masters to employ a certain number of journeymen. Sometimes the Government confessed its blunders with a winning frankness unusual in modern times. After the Peace with Holland in 1654, it was noticed with pleasure that men could earn 16*d.* a day, and could "live without being soldiers." A theory which finds favour with some modern reformers, seems to have prevailed in the seventeenth century, that the competition of immigrants from the rural districts brought down the wages of town artisans, and deprived them of employment, and numerous attempts were made to prevent the movement. Debarred by the property qualifications from the practice of many handicrafts, and confined to their parishes by the laws of settlement, the agricultural labourers destroyed one another by a disastrous competition. Yet many eluded the vigilance of the parish authorities, and escaped to the towns, where it is to be feared they scarcely improved their prospects. But there is reason to believe that insecurity and irregularity of employment were the normal conditions under which artisans and agricultural labourers worked during the seventeenth century. If we may suppose any equivalence between the yearly and daily rates which were sometimes given in the same assessment, it is impossible to believe that the artisan in any industry could reckon on continuous employment for 300 days. The average was more probably between 200 and 260.

This impression is strengthened by a further examin ation of the conditions of industry. First of all there was a closer interdependence between agriculture and industry in England than there is at the present time. The abolition of the Corn Laws, and the perfecting of ocean-going steamers have made the yield of an English harvest of relatively small importance. Compared with the seventeenth century, we can treat the price of provisions as almost constant. But in the seventeenth century, and for 140 years afterwards, the condition of agriculture was the principal factor in the situation. The clumsy and old-fashioned system which prevailed, and which in the main withstood the efforts of pamphleteers and practical reformers, during the period before us, was the secret of the slow development of English industry. The alternate expansion and restriction of demand for manufactured goods, the rapid fluctuations in the prices of these commodities, must be traced to the influence of the seasons. The long series of bad or deficient harvests in the seventeenth century must have involved a great deal of disturbance in the general industry of the country, and flung hundreds of craftsmen temporarily into the ranks of the unemployed. While this economical interdependence between industry and agriculture was more clearly marked than it is at the present time, there was not so distinct a line of demarcation between the practice of agriculture and handicraft. In the small country towns and the rural districts they overlapped, especially in the earlier stages of manufacture. So the harvest involved considerable interruption in the industrial life of the people. In the textile trades, much of the spinning was done in the country cottages, even when the weavers worked in town conditions. The harvest demand for agricultural labour in these circumstances stopped the spinning-wheel, and necessarily brought a time of slackness or enforced idleness on the weavers. In one district indeed a legal sanction was given to this practice by the Act "for regulating and making stuffs in Norfolk and Norwich" (13 & 14 Car. II. c. 5, 1662), by which it was provided, that "whereas the custom hath been retained time out of mind, and found expedient that there should be a cessation of weaving every year in the time of Harvest, in regard the spinners of yarn which the said weavers do use are at that time chiefly employed in Harvest work," no weaver should set any loom at work from August 15th to September 15th, on pain of forfeiting 40*s*. for every loom used within that period.

§ 7. *Bye-industries.*

This raises the question of bye-industries, using the expression in the sense of any secondary means of increasing the earnings of the family. The weaving and spinning which went on in the cottages in the rural districts was at first secondary in importance to the agricultural labour, the cultivation of a little land, and the use of common rights of pasture which it supplemented. Here no apprenticeship was necessary, and the payment by piece was miserably low. At the end of the book will be found the Lancashire and other rates for weaving, collected from Thorold

Rogers' sixth volume. Spinning was remunerated at rates lower still. It will be seen that the cottage weaving here noted was confined to the commonest woollen and linen goods. But we early meet with attempts to stop the extension of the system to broad cloth, and to confine it to production for family needs alone. In 1662 a fine of £5 per month was imposed for every month that "he, she, or they" should, without apprenticeship, make broad cloth to sell. But it is doubtful whether any serious interruption to the process was the result. Certainly no one could have benefited from the competition of this cheap cottage labour. The people in the northern counties were less civilized, and had a lower standard of comfort than the other textile districts. It is possible that the cottage weavers gained some temporary benefit from the extension of the domestic system. But in the long run only the dealer gained. Division of labour also was not carried so far in the seventeenth century, and many craftsmen must have eked out the earnings from the practice of their recognized trade, by tacking on some of the subsidiary branches, or cognate industries. Thus we find artisans practising wool-combing and weaving, brewing and dyeing, sieve-making and thread-making, etc.; while women were spinsters, and also made bonelace and thread.

§ 8. *The Agricultural Labourers.*

There is one other qualification of importance which we must make to the general statement of the condition of the working-classes in the seventeenth century—that is, the gradual falling off of the agricultural labourer relative to the artisans. At the beginning of the period under review, there was not that great difference between the two classes of labour which is such a marked feature of the last forty years, and the 200 years which have since elapsed. Allowing for the numerous advantages the skilled agricultural labourer had over the town artisan in the rights of common, the garden, or the bit of land he cultivated, there is really not much to choose between him and the second-class carpenter or bricklayer, while his lot was preferable to that of the ordinary journeyman craftsman. But this state of things very soon altered. It is not clearly marked in the first forty years (1583—1622). Indeed, in some districts, the wages of agriculture increased, while wages in the building trades were stationary. All classes shared in the rise between 1623 and 1662, but the agricultural labourer's lot shows a much lower rate of improvement than that of the other trades; while, after 1662, agricultural wages are altogether stationary, or increase at an almost imperceptible rate. The object of the Government appears to have been to stop the immigration of labourers from the rural districts, in the interests of the craftsmen. They adopted the strange method of confining them to their parishes, reducing them to poverty, and then supplying pauper apprentices to compete with the craftsmen.

§ 9. *Trading and Industrial Classes.*

Traces of the manufacturing system have been found by Dr. Cunningham in the sixteenth century, and in the seventeenth the advantages of the division of labour were widely recognized. In the towns there was a combination of the domestic with the manufacturing system, *i.e.* certain operations were carried on by handicraftsmen grouped together in workshops or factories, while subsidiary processes were performed in the homes of the people. In the more rural districts, the usual industrial group was the family. The dealer gave out raw material to be worked up by the craftsman and his wife and children. But there was no deep line of division between dealer and artisan, or merchant and employer. At one end of the scale was the merchant, who would probably be a member of a trading company—the "economic man" of the mercantilists—and at the other, the simple journeyman craftsman. But midway between these was a large class whose functions in the industrial system overlapped each other, and cannot easily be separated. We find (1) the master craftsman, with his journeyman and apprentices, purchasing his own raw material and selling the product to the dealer; (2) the master craftsman working up with the aid of journeymen and apprentices the raw material which was given out by the dealer; (3) the master craftsman acting also in the capacity of dealer; (4) the simple dealer in finished commodities; (5) the dealer, with craftsmen working on his own premises under his supervision; (6) women and children working independently for the dealer, or assisting the husband or father; (7) any of these combining his ordinary functions with a retail trade, and sometimes with agriculture.

§ 10. *A Craftsman's Life.*

To make this picture of seventeenth century industrial relations more vivid, it may be well to recall some incidents in the life of a craftsman sixty or seventy years ago, in one of the Staffordshire domestic industries—hinge-manufacturing. At that time, and indeed till only twenty years ago, the system had been almost unaffected by the introduction o machinery. One could still find boys apprenticed to th craft in the usual form, and it is easy to recall the lit shop standing in the large garden, surrounded with old-fashioned garden flowers, and the pile of coke outside the workshop door. The shop itself had wooden shutters and roof, but no further protection from rain and wind. The floor was the bare earth, and there was many a hole in the walls. But it had its old associations. Here the craftsman's father had worked before him, with two or three apprentices, whom he had many a time threatened with leather-apron for neglect of duty. The craftsman bought his own iron, finished his hinges, packed them, and conveyed them to the warehouse of the factor in the large town, who bought them for the price agreed upon. Let us recall the incidents of his life. Seventy years ago, our hingemaker is what in the old days would have been called a journeyman. He has the reputation of a good workman, but he has fallen in bad times, and he has no employment, no capital, and no business connection. But he contrives to get on, as we shall see. His great chance is a small order he has obtained from the factor in the neighbouring town, which he has to complete within a given time. He obtains a sufficient quantity of iron on credit from the dealer. He then borrows tools and standing-room in the shop of a friend, already set up in business. In this manner he completes the order, takes his goods to the factor, and receives payment. Other orders follow, which he fulfils in his neighbour's shop, making a small payment for the use of it until he can build and stock one of his own. He then extends his business, and takes apprentices, still working for the same factor. Life apparently goes as merrily as can be. He marries, and as his boys grow up, he trains some of hem in the craft. But the connection with the town factor which he relies for his living is very flimsy. Competition is remorseless, even under the old system; and the hinge-maker's business comes near extinction when a rival, maybe a near kinsman, gets the trade by offering to manufacture the hinges a little cheaper. He then has a period of great trial, and practically has to begin over again. Finally, he leaves a diminished trade to his eldest son, which flickers on for many years, managed on exactly the same principles. The hinge-maker has all the freedom the loss of which the modern workman so regrets—freedom to work from fifteen to eighteen hours a day, in a stifling little shop, for bare subsistence, and to be driven to the wall by the stress of competition from rivals. It must not be forgotten, however, that the large garden supplies a valuable addition to the resources of the family. It more than suffices for their own needs, and leaves a surplus to be sent to market.

In the same district there were many similar industries, managed on the same system, except that occasionally the master became very much like the modern capitalist employer, with numerous journeymen working in his large workshop for weekly wages. Sixty years ago, when there were farm-houses and a fairy well where now the railway station stands, and pleasant fields where now one hears only the thud of the steam-hammer, there had been little or no change in these industries since the seventeenth or early part of the eighteenth century.

§ 11. *Abuses.*

The ordinary journeyman in the seventeenth century had great difficulty in obtaining a good start in life if he was friendless and had no capital. That this was his general condition seems highly probable. He could not save on the wages he received, and the close personal relation between master and man, which is popularly supposed to have been such a beneficent feature of the old system, was probably not usual. The sentiments entertained by the craftsmen themselves towards the master-clothiers is well reflected in the ballad of the end of the seventeenth century quoted by Macaulay, where one of the latter is made to say—

> "In former ages we used to give,
> So that our workfolks like farmers did live;
> But the times are changed; we will make them know.
> * * * * * *
> We will make them to work hard for sixpence a day,
> Though a shilling they deserve if they had their just pay;
> If at all they murmur and say 'tis too small,
> We bid them choose whether they'll work at all.
> And thus we do gain all our wealth and estate,
> By many poor men that work early and late.
> Then hey for the clothing trade! It goes on brave;
> We scorn for to toyl and moyl, nor yet to slave.
> Our workmen do work hard, but we live at ease;
> We go when we will, and we come when we please."

There was a very general custom during the seventeenth century, and indeed before that time, which became a powerful means of oppression and extortion in the hands of unscrupulous employers of labour. It has since been almost extinguished by the Truck Acts, though it is still a source of evil in the survivals of the domestic industries, where it is extremely difficult to secure a strict observance of the law. The truck system was the natural result of clinging to old customs in changed conditions of industry where the ancient relation between employer and employed no longer existed. It is not within the scope of this work to trace the changes in the methods of payment of wages. The truck system was after all only one form of payment in kind, which in the Middle Ages appears to have been general, and was probably innocent enough. That the truck system was an evil as early as the days of Edward IV. is evident from the statute on the subject quoted by Dr. Cunningham. The domestic system, under which the dealer or the factor was master of the lives and fortunes of the working-classes, must have aggravated an evil which it was peculiarly fitted to encourage. Under the domestic system the interests of the middleman combined with the weakness and poverty of the workers to degrade what had been an innocent custom into a grave abuse. We find many attempts, during the seventeenth century, to grapple with the evil, which was rife in the staple industries in the country. Allusion has already been made to one attempt in 1604, which affected the hardware trades. It will be sufficient to quote one Act of Parliament (1 Ann. sess. 1, stat. 2, c. 18, 1701), which indicates how widespread the evil had become, and at the same time attempts to check it. Clause 3 of this statute recites that "to prevent the oppression of the labourers and workmen employed in the woollen, linen, fustian, cotton, and iron manufacture . . . . all payments and satisfactions hereafter to be made to any of the same labourers and workmen for any work by them done in the same manufacture, shall be by the lawful coin of this realm, and not by any cloth, victuals, or commodities in lieu thereof." There are other Acts of Parliament to the same effect. That the evil grew during the eighteenth and early part of the nineteenth century is well-known. It is curious to observe that just as the domestic system made it possible for this abuse to obtain a firm hold on the industrial community, so it is in the survivals of that system that it has not yet altogether relaxed its hold. Factory organization, the Truck Acts, and the Trade Union have released the workers from this form of oppression.

The workers in the seventeenth century suffered also from the competition of pauper apprentices. The Act 7 Jac. I. c. 2, recites that "forasmuch as the true labour and exercise of husbandry, and the bringing up of apprentices of both sexes in trades and manual occupations is a good thing for the community, and great sums of money has been given to various cities for this purpose—the binding apprentice of the poorest sort of children unto needful trades and occupations; the experience whereof hath brought forth very great profit and commodity unto those cities, towns, and parishes, where any parts of the said monies have been so given and employed." "Without such attention, the poorer sorts of children would be brought up in idleness." "Where suitably poor children are not in the parish where the money is, the poorest children from an adjoining parish may be so apprenticed."

§ 12. *The Employment of Women.*

The extensive employment of women and children in industry does not date from the introduction of the factory system. The very essence of the domestic system was the employment of the *family*. Not only the head of the household, but his wife and children took part in the work which supported all. Now this system, in its purest form, was open to the same objections that can be urged against domestic industries in our own day. The women and children's labour was simply subsidiary to that of the head of the household. They were either not separately paid at all, *i. e.* the master workman received what was supposed to be adequate remuneration for the labour of the whole family; their wages were simply included in a vague manner in the earnings of the household; or, when the women and children, working in no direct relation to the head of the household, did spinning, winding, etc. in their homes, they were paid at a miserably low rate. That this system led to the gravest abuses is evident from numerous statutes, which indicate low wages for all concerned. Thus in 17 Jac. I. c. 7, we have an Act "for punishing and correcting deceit and frauds committed by sorters, kembers, spinsters of wool, and weavers of woollen yarn." It complains of the embezzlement of the cloths, yarn, etc., given out by the clothier, "to the great damage of the clothier." "Many exercising the trades aforesaid are greatly impoverished; and the parties which commit the offences, being poor and altogether unable to make recompense or satisfaction for the trespasses .... have much discouraged the said clothier to set poor people on work, whereby much poverty doth increase, and more is like daily to increase." Those unable to make restitution in the form prescribed by the Justices were to be apprehended and whipped, or set in the stocks. The domestic employment of women and children in the seventeenth century was very general. This can be easily seen from the statutes made for the regulation of various trades. In 1662 an Act was passed prohibiting the importation of foreign bonelace, cut work, embroidery, fringe, band strings, button and needlework. These home trades "set on work many poor children, and other persons who have very small means or maintenance of living, other than by their labours and endeavours in the said art." Again, in 1698, an Act was passed "to prevent the making or selling buttons made of cloth, serge, drugget, or other stuffs." "The maintenance and subsistence of many thousands of men, women, and children within this kingdom depends upon the making of silk, mohair, gimp, and thread-buttons with the needle, and great numbers of throwsters, twisters, spinners, winders, dyers, and others are employed in preparing the materials of which such buttons are made."

The employment of women and children was not confined to the home industries. Indeed, there could be no reason for supposing that as the custom grew of grouping together bodies of workers in factories, the women and children would be left to work in their homes. They would naturally be drawn into the general system. The references to the advantages of division of labour, which we find in the pamphlets of the period, and to the employment of women and children, can only be explained on this hypothesis. The preamble of a statute for regulating silk-throwing (1662) states that the company of silk-throwers employed more than 40,000 men, women, and children, who otherwise would unavoidably be burthensome to the places of abode. Clause 9 provides that "it shall and may be lawful to and for any Freeman of the said Company of Silk-throwers, to set on work and employ any person or persons, being native subjects to his Majesty, and no others, whether they be men, women, or children, to turn the mill, tie threads, double silk, and wind silk, as formerly they have used to do, although such persons . . . . have not been bred up as apprentices for seven years." The Company of Silk-throwers were not to have the power of fixing wages, which were to be settled, presumably, by competition by employers and employed. Six years afterwards, the master silk-throwers complained that the Company tried to prevent freemen from working more than 160 spindles, and assistants 240 spindles at the same time, to the great hindrance of the trade; and the Company was disabled for the future from making any bye-law limiting the number of "mills, spindles, and other utensils."

The effect of the domestic system on women's wages has been great. It can be seen that, roughly speaking, men and women in industry have very different historical antecedents. Until the sixteenth century, the industrial employment of women came under four heads. The majority of the women of the working-class were probably engaged in the bye-industries to supply the necessities of the home, and in certain agricultural operations. We find them also in the building trades, and that they practised handicraft is evident from the gild regulations concerning women members, and from the mention of them in Acts of Parliament. In some of the gilds and chartered companies they were treated on practically equal terms with the men. But, generally speaking, women's labour was domestic and subsidiary to that of the head of the family. There is no trace of a *class* of women wholly dependent for subsistence on their own exertions, their labour co-extensive and equal in importance with that of men. The greater division of labour and the extension of the domestic system provided new outlets for women's labour which had not before existed. That system was essentially fitted for absorbing the energies of the women and children of the family. The employment of women and children on a large scale dates evidently from the seventeenth century, and then they were employed for the most part only in branches in which they could become efficient without much difficulty. This development found women without any organization, without traditions of apprenticeship and skilled work. Thousands of women and children probably worked in the domestic shop, and helped to swell the earnings of the father without ever seeing the money-equivalent for their labour. Putting on one side the gild system, about which, so far as it affected women's employment, very little is known, we may safely say that it is only in modern times that the conception of woman as a separate, independent worker has been reached. By the majority she is still regarded as simply the helpmate of man; and this historical factor in the determination of women's wages is still of the utmost importance.

§ 13. *Foreign Immigrants.*

In the chapter on the Monopolies we pointed out the great value of the patent lists in throwing light on the economic development of the seventeenth century. In the history of inventions indeed is contained the whole genesis and development of the modern industrial system, and nothing more clearly shows the gradual character of industrial change. We hear of some famous invention which has apparently at one blow transformed a great industry, and we are apt to forget the slow modifications which have taken place beforehand. But it will be found that in almost every case the great invention has been preceded by others of less importance, which may sometimes be counted by hundreds. After long lapse of time and patient and often unrequited labour of many men, the minute transforming forces are combined and brought to a focus in some great invention, and the old methods, after carrying on a fruitless struggle with the new, finally succumb. People frequently speak as though there had been no mechanical inventions until the latter half of the eighteenth century; that then, within a very few years the whole industrial system was suddenly transformed by some half-dozen discoveries; and that ever since we have been merely adapting ourselves to conditions then introduced. The sixteenth and the seventeenth centuries were not unfertile in inventions. They have been dwarfed by the more important discoveries of a later day, and when we study the inventions of the eighteenth century we unconsciously allow conceptions derived from the industrial system of our own times to mislead us in forming an estimate of their importance. So our view of industrial development is distorted. We do not see the modifications of the industrial system in their true perspective. One useful method of eliminating error in our observations is to return to the sixteenth and seventeenth centuries, where we find on a smaller scale analogous changes. Riots against new machines, statutes aiming at the preservation of old methods, petitions from bodies of workers who felt their means of livelihood endangered, complaints against the French and Flemish immigrants who introduced many new processes, and the patent lists themselves, all indicate transition, and loss to some classes. For example, the makers of woollen caps find themselves "impoverished" by the "excessive use of hats and felts," and (1565) a statute is levelled against the fulling mills "to set poor and impotent people on work." The Devonshire clothiers (1593) complain that the Devonshire kersies are "discredited by the inventions and new devices of the weavers, tuckers, and artificers." The card-makers and card-wire drawers of London, Bristol, Gloucester, Norwich, and Coventry obtained, in 1597, an Act against the new foreign cards for wool. The people in the North complain of the new engines for stretching and tentering cloth, a grievance which occurs again later on. In 1695 we hear of riots amongst the silk-weavers against the new "engines."

But one of the most enduring and far-reaching influences in English industry in the seventeenth century was the immigration of French and Flemish refugees. There was a constant influx of foreigners from the middle of the sixteenth to the end of the seventeenth century, the greatest numbers coming over at the time of the sack of Antwerp in 1583, and before and after the Revocation of the Edict of Nantes; and England is largely indebted to them for the development of her home industries and for improvements in agriculture. They entered practically every trade, though the largest numbers are found in the textile industries. The English Government consistently favoured these immigrants, fully alive to the advantages of affording a refuge to the skilled workmen of Flanders and France. Allusion has already been made to the privileges conferred on them by the suspension of statutes and municipal bye-laws in their favour. The settlement of the Walloons in the Eastern Counties is said to have revived the prosperity of Norwich, Colchester, and other eastern towns, where before their arrival it is asserted that there was actually a proposal to pull down the public buildings, so great was the decay of trade! Many indemnities and the free use of churches and the exercise of their religion were granted to them by Edward VI. We find foreign immigrants in 1571 in London, where there were 4,631; Colchester, Harwich, Ipswich, Yarmouth, Norwich, the Cinque Ports, Southampton, Boston, Canterbury, Maidstone, and other towns. They introduced the bay and say trade at Sandwich, the silk at Canterbury, and the thread at Maidstone. The foreign immigrants, however, aroused the hostility of native craftsmen and merchants, though restrictions upon them were unpopular with the mass of the people. Complaints were made that they did not submit to the regulations to which English artificers were subjected, that their presence enhanced house-rent and the prices of provisions, that they undersold native traders by their cheap labour, and objections were raised to the new mechanical methods which the foreigners introduced.

Many attempts were made to restrict the employment of foreigners in the reign of James I., and encouragement was given to native industries, but the measures adopted did not seriously interfere with the immigrants. Religious animosity in the time of Charles I. was a more serious evil, and the mistaken zeal of Bishop Wren of Norwich drove many of them away. At the time of the Revocation of the Edict of Nantes the number of refugees greatly increased. They were encouraged by Charles II., and though James II. seconded the efforts of Louis XIV. to recall to their own country those who had been its strength, very few returned to France. They introduced the manufacture of sail cloth, lute string, and other industries, and improved the silk trade, which became one of the most important of English industries, while Lyons, its old centre, declined. The presence of the French refugees partly inspired the prohibitive tariffs on French goods in the reign of William III., and it is interesting to notice that the petitions against the free trade clauses of the Treaty of Utrecht came mainly from the industries which had received a large accession of French refugees.

There is another feature of seventeenth century industrial history which is worthy of notice, the migration of the staple industries of the country. The manufacture of cloth in the east and west and midland counties continued to be of considerable importance until the era of the industrial revolution, but during the seventeenth century the progress of textile industries in the north threatened the older centres of the trade. The rapid extension of the cloth trade in the north is evident from the statutes made for its regulation. The iron trade of Staffordshire and the Forest of Dean, and the numberless small industries dependent on it, was also growing at this time, and much attention was given to mining. These new developments, small as they were compared with those of a later day, undoubtedly stimulated population (though we have no reliable statistics of its movement), whether we accept Professor Rogers' calculation that the population of the country doubled during the seventeenth century, or Mr. Rickman's more moderate estimate based on the death-rate.

§ 14. *Industrial System of the Seventeenth Century.*

The industrial system which we have been reviewing was very favourable to the growth of a large class of middlemen. A system of small domestic workshops, and manufactories differing scarcely at all from them, scattered over wide districts; the necessity of warehousing goods for some time; the concentration of the export trade in the hands of certain privileged merchants; the limitation of the trade to a few ports; poor means of communication and of transport by land—these were conditions in which the middleman became a useful and necessary member of society. With the increase of trade in the eighteenth century, the number of middlemen necessarily increased. But the "great industry" of modern times is unfavourable to this class. Types familiar enough years ago are rapidly vanishing before the consolidating and economizing influences of extreme competition and improved means of communication. It is a common saying in some parts of the country: "Ah! their days are over: they will never again make large fortunes." Ordinary people long ago realized by practical experience the idea of industrial evolution. The changes which took place between 1760 and 1825 stimulated trade and population in an unprecedented degree, but it is necessary to remember that the new system was not suddenly imposed on the whole industry of the country. The factory system has been gradually extended to one industry after another. Many industries are still substantially unchanged; in others the substitution is taking place. But the change of system has been slow, and for sixty years was unaccompanied by any great improvement in the means of communication. The perfecting of the railway system, the penny post, the telegraph and the telephone were necessary to the completion of the industrial revolution.

In the seventeenth century the dealer or the factor was master of the lives and fortunes of the working-classes. He had them completely in his power. If they refused to accept his terms, he could break the connection to which they looked for their subsistence. In spite of the Acts to which allusion has been made, he could fix the mode of payment. He might coerce the workers into accepting goods they did not want, in lieu of money wages; and after keeping them at starvation point, he might have them whipped or set in the stocks for embezzling cloth or other goods entrusted to them, which they hoped to sell for food. There were no doubt bright features in the domestic system; probably many a connection between dealer and worker, which scarce anything short of a complete change of system could shake, passed on from father to son. Many a craftsman could say of his employer, that "he had worked for the family since he was a lad, as his father had done before him." This was the case not so long ago in many domestic industries, and is so still in some of the most degraded survivals. But such a personal attachment to an old employer is only beneficial when it is not palmed off for current coin of the realm, and when it is the spontaneous outcome of mutual respect and affection. If the workman serves a bad employer, his affections may easily become his ruin. He does not like to resist what may be an unjust reduction of wages or try to obtain a too-long-delayed rise. He drifts along, a willing and patient slave to the greed of a man not worthy of his attachment. The cash *nexus* is a very unsatisfactory bond between employer and workman, but it is a necessary preliminary to a nobler connection, and it is better than the personal relation of the domestic system, for it has made trade union action possible.

While the dealer was in this strong position, the working-classes on the other hand were weaker and more isolated than had ever been before or than they have been since. We hear, it is true, of associations of journeymen, but, generally speaking, the workers had no organization, and few interests in common. The law did not protect them. It was indeed illegal for them to take the only course—the formation of trade unions, which would have been a protection against employers. It is evident from what has been said about Stat. 5 Eliz., that while the apprenticeship clauses may to a certain extent have restricted competition, their general tendency was hostile to the interests of the majority of the workers. The possible benefit of the apprenticeship regulations was more than neutralized by the clauses in the Act empowering Justices of the Peace or other town magistrates to fix wages. How this worked has been seen. It gave the working-classes into the hands of landlords and employers. It is true that the amendment (1 Jac. I. c. 6) forbade Justices of the Peace who were clothiers to fix the wages of weavers. The fact that this provision was considered necessary shows how the statute was abused, and a similar protection was not extended to other trades.

The numerous statutes passed for the regulation of industry aimed rather at securing a certain quality in the manufactures than the protection of the worker. Allusion has been made to some statutes for guarding against the abuses of the truck system, but even these must have been virtually inoperative for lack of efficient inspection. Few workmen would have dared to inform against the dealer or the employer. He might have been fined, but the result to the worker would have been loss of employment. The humanitarian ideas of State interference, which are so potent an influence in modern times, were not the basis of seventeenth century legislation. In the wide field covered by Acts of Parliament restricting the employment of women and children, enforcing good sanitation, and maintaining the legal rights of the labourers, there was, in the seventeenth century and in the years preceding, complete *laissez faire*. State interference, in the modern sense of the words, is a comparatively recent movement. It is of great importance to bear this in mind in criticizing economic theory. Many people have justified their hostility to the Factory Acts and similar legislation by appealing to the teaching of the *laissez faire* school of economists. The latter, by pushing too far a theory suggested by circumstances peculiar to the eighteenth century, and which, strictly interpreted, covers only a narrow range of social phenomena, have supplied the opponents of State interference with strong arguments. But if we trace the history of the *laissez faire* system to its source in the revolt against foolish attempts to direct industry into artificial channels, high protective tariffs, close trade corporations, and unwise restrictions on the free movement of labour, there is little in English political economy to cause uneasiness to the upholders of factory legislation and other methods of State regulation of labour in modern times.

§ 15. *The First Half of the Eighteenth Century.*

The eighteenth century opened with a succession of bad seasons, which checked though they did not altogether stop that upward movement which has been pointed out. The years 1693—1700 were known as "the seven barren years of the seventeenth century," though they were by no means so unpropitious as some others in that period. The purchasing power of wages diminished from 1694 to 1698, but increased in the following year, although eleven out of the twenty-three seasons, from 1692 to 1715, were more or less deficient in produce.

The next fifty years present many difficulties. It seems clear that the working-classes entered on a period of greater prosperity, and were able to live in greater comfort than they had enjoyed for a century and a half, but it is not easy to estimate the extent of the improvement. During Walpole's long administration the country made rapid progress. His financial ability, his free-trade measures, and his peaceful policy stimulated manufactures and commerce, and this movement was maintained after his fall in 1742. The favourable seasons which commenced in 1715 continued with little interruption till 1765, when a change set in from plenty to dearth.

Defoe's description of the clothing trade in the West Riding is well known, and it has served to strengthen the favourable impression conveyed by other facts of the condition of the working-classes at this time. "Tho' we met few People without Doors, yet within we saw the Houses full of lusty Fellows, some at the Dye-vat, some at the Loom, others dressing the Cloths; the Women and Children carding or spinning; all employed from the youngest to the oldest, scarce anything above four years old, but its hands were sufficient for its own Support. Not a Beggar to be seen, not an idle Person, except here and there in an Almshouse, built for those that are ancient and past working. The People in general live long; they enjoy a good Air, and under such Circumstances hard Labour is naturally attended with the double Blessing both of Health and Riches." Defoe seems to have been more impressed with the woollen trade of the north, where it was rapidly growing, than with that of the eastern and western counties. He visited Yorkshire and Lancashire three times to acquaint himself with their manufactures. But interesting as his remarks are, he tells us little that we desire to know. His account is the impression of a man passing rapidly through the country, and seizing upon the external characteristics which met his view. It contains no exact information about wages, hours of labour, the sanitary condition of the people, or the relations between employers and employed; and he regards manufactures from the point of view of a seventeenth century pamphleteer, as a means of giving employment to the poor. Statistically, his observations are of little or no value. The most interesting remark is that relating to the employment of women and children. We should like to know how far the evils complained of in the statutes of Anne to George I., the embezzlement of materials by the poor workers, the truck system, etc., prevailed in the West Riding when Defoe went on his tours.

Many writers—Voltaire, the author of the *Corn Tracts*, Adam Smith, Malthus, Hallam, Tooke, Thorold Rogers, etc. —have commented favourably on the condition of the working-classes during the reign of George II. The general impression conveyed is that they had a greater command of the necessaries of life than they had enjoyed either earlier in the eighteenth or in the seventeenth century. "Bread made of wheat became more generally the food of the labouring people." Malthus experienced some difficulty in explaining the phenomena of this period in accordance with his theory. "It will evidently be the average earnings of the families of the labouring-classes throughout the year on which the encouragement to marriage and the power of supporting children will depend, and not merely the wages of day-labour estimated in food." He then points out that from 1735 to 1755, a day's labour would on an average purchase a peck of wheat, but implies that this relatively high rate of wages was counterbalanced by a less constant demand for labour and greater irregularity of employment than the working-classes experienced between 1790 and 1811. He thus explains "the more rapid increase of population in the latter period, in perfect consistency with the general principle." But this explanation is unsatisfactory. It is open to the objection that it avoids the difficulty by denying its existence. In order to understand the significance of the period under discussion, it is necessary to compare it with that which preceded and with that which followed it. Now the growth of population during the first half of the seventeenth century, when the working-classes suffered from continuous distress, and were forced down to a lower standard of comfort, was very rapid, if we adopt only the moderate calculations of Mr. Rickman. The improvement during the latter half of the century, which was maintained up to and during the reign of George II., has been pointed out. But the increase in population during this period was extremely slow—from 5,773,646 in 1670 to 6,517,035 in 1750, according to Rickman's calculations. During the reign of George II. there appears to have been a slightly accelerated rate of increase. The reasons which Malthus considered a satisfactory explanation of the rapid increase after 1770 have no weight when we discuss the first half of the seventeenth century. But in some respects there is an analogy between the two periods. In both the working-classes reverted to a lower standard of comfort—in both of them the seasons were almost continuously unfavourable, in both the purchasing power of wages was exceptionally low. Thus between two periods of great trial for the working-classes, during which population rapidly increased, we have a third period of relative prosperity during which they reached and maintained a higher level of comfort, and which apparently retarded rather than encouraged the growth of population. A review of the seventeenth and eighteenth centuries points to the principle that below a certain level a further deterioration of the standard of comfort stimulates the growth of population.

§ 16. *The Gloucestershire Weavers in* 1756.

Although the argument of Malthus does not explain the slow growth of population during the reign of George II. compared with other periods, and the condition of the working-classes really shows a considerable improvement, there is no reason for thinking that this period was free from the drawbacks which have been pointed out in the seventeenth century. Those familiar with the pleasing characteristics which a few years ago might have been seen on a hasty progress through villages engaged in domestic industries, will be on their guard against the conclusions suggested by the vague descriptions of writers like Defoe. The narrative of the proceedings in Gloucestershire, which led up to the Clothiers' Petition of 1757, throws some light on the condition of the weavers in that county. It was written to support the case of the employers, and therefore would not be likely to exaggerate the evils of which the weavers complained. It is interesting also as an account of a strike in the eighteenth century, and as one of the first attempts to obtain the repeal of the Statute of Apprenticeship.

The narrative states that the clothiers desire relief from certain grievances and impediments to which the trade is subjected, and which encourage "commotions." "Many idle and dissolute fellows, never bred up to the weaving trade, finding the advantage of such a disguise, have styled themselves journeyman weavers, and rambled about the country to a considerable distance, exacting alms under that denomination." The "original sources of the commotions" are stated to have been "the decay of trade, the intemperance and bad economy of the labouring manufacturers in general, and the increase of the number of weavers in proportion to other workmen employed. To this may be added the dearness of provisions." It must be remembered that these are the statements of the clothiers. They complain of French competition, and allege that want of employment is the chief ground of the weavers' complaints. They attribute their evils to the want of economy, the luxurious style of living, and especially the intemperance of "the labouring manufacturers." Their bad economy is shown by the fact that they do not go to market for common necessaries, but "buy them at the worst hand at huckster's shops." They do not bake their own bread, "but eat bakers', the whitest and most delicate that can be made." The clothiers attribute the increase in the number of weavers to the practice of apprenticing paupers to that trade. "The master weavers will take them younger and cheaper, and will provide for them."

The weavers, however, attributed their evils to the disuse of the custom of fixing wages at the Quarter Sessions. There was an assessment in force, which had been drawn up in 1727 (*vide* Appendix), but some of the clothiers made separate contracts with their weavers, who, they said, were well satisfied with their then wages, and agreed to work upon the same terms as long as they were employed by their respective masters. The dissatisfaction of the weavers, however, at last led to violent outbreaks. Threatening letters, of which the following is a specimen, were sent to the clothiers denouncing the separate contracts: "To Mr. Thomas Roberts, post-paid.—This is to give notice to all weavers not to put their hands to any paper made by Mr. Roberts or any other clothier, if you do, we the weavers of each parish are fully resolved to meet in a body and car him on the wooden horse, and throw him into his master's mill-pond where he sign'd the wrighting. And as for you clothiers, we think it not worth your whiles to trouble yourselves with any such thing, if you do, be it to your peril, though it is our desire to be at quiet."

The weavers of one employer voluntarily signed agreements, whereupon the other weavers waited upon Mr. Stephens, one of the Justices, and desired his advice in order to prevent private contracts. He informed them that "unless these contracts were put a stop to, their Act of Parliament was of no value." Supported by this magisterial statement, the strikers coerced the blacklegs. They informed the offending clothier that the Justices were on their side, whereupon he thought it best to send for the principal weavers in his employ, and destroy the contract in their presence.

The whole matter was referred to the Justices at the Michaelmas Quarter Sessions, 1756. The weavers presented a petition expressing their satisfaction with the Wages Assessment of 1727. They complained that the clothiers treated it with contempt, "well knowing that this court could not inflict any penalty on the non-conformance therewith, and that the weavers could not bear the expense of applying to this court for any breach thereof." They said they "could not get above fourpence for sixteen hours' labour upon many sorts of work," complained of the "hardships and oppressions" of the clothiers who reduced wages, and the laws against combinations, and petitioned the Justices to fix wages in conformity with the Acts. The clothiers, on the other hand, argued against the Act. They said that it raised the price of labour, and so was prejudicial to the trade of the nation, which was suffering from foreign competition. "The execution of this law tends to invert the laws of society, and to destroy that due subordination which ought to be religiously preserved in all communities." The various sorts of weaving could not be reduced to a regular or fixed standard. "These and all other laws for the regulation of the price of labour are not to be reduced to practice, nor expedient to be put into execution. . . . There need be no better evidence of this than to consider how many of them lie dormant at this time, notwithstanding they are not repealed." The present rate of wages was sufficient; a single loom could get from 13*s.* to 15*s.* a week. "Weavers who work under their own roofs were not exposed to those hardships and difficulties which many other trades were liable to . . . . the weak, the lame, the old and decrepid, the puny women, and even children, and such whose constitutions and natural abilities were not equal to other employments, were made weavers." They contended that it was impossible to rate the price of weaving by the hundred, and that the execution of the law would tend "to injure the goodness of the manufactory." They thought it "absolutely absurd and repugnant to the liberties of a free people and the interest of trade that any law should supersede a private contract honourably made between a master and his workman." The execution of the law would lead to the migration of the manufacture. "The county of Suffolk and some other places were formerly the seats of manufacture for woollen broadcloths, where it is now hardly known. Salisbury and Worcester were celebrated within the last century for the same, till, under the mistaken notion of wise regulations and salutary restrictions, and through the grants of particular privileges, freedoms, and exclusive charters, they have driven it from them; and

Yorkshire, within our own knowledge, hath gained from us some considerable branches of our trade, because their labouring manufacturers are better economists, more tractable, temperate, and frugal, and consequently work cheaper than ours."

The evidence of the clothiers was said to establish two points, (1) that the wages of the weavers had not been reduced for many years, and that one loom could earn from 13*s.* to 18*s.* and even 21*s.* a week; (2) that the regulation of wages by the hundred was impracticable in an equitable manner, because the clothier or the weaver must frequently be injured by it. Further evidence was given of the wages actually paid. The average for a single loom appeared to be from £35 to £40 per annum. One clothier, however, paid upwards of £45, and to a weaver who kept two looms at work and employed neither journeyman nor apprentice but only his own family, £95 14*s.* for work done in one year and a day over. A second employer had paid nearly £80 in a year to a weaver who worked two looms with the aid of his family; while a third had paid £50 to a weaver for one loom. The clothiers maintained that the lowest prices per hundred were sometimes the best wages, and that the introduction of the "bobbing-shuttle" within the last twenty years enabled the weaver to do the same amount of work one day in eight sooner than was before possible. They admitted that some instances of low and oppressive wages might have occurred, but they contended that these low wages deserved less notice than was expected. The wages of the *loom* had to be divided amongst those who worked at it. "It appeared, in the course of the weavers' evidence, that the persons employed to work one single loom were the master, a journeyman, and a child for a quill-winder, who is commonly entitled to 1*d*. out of the shilling; that often the wife or daughter, or an apprentice boy, from twelve to fifteen years of age, acts the part of a journeyman, who is entitled to one-third of the whole wages for such a piece of work, besides small beer and lodging (if he has no home of his own); that sometimes a journeyman works at the head of a loom, with an apprentice boy; in which case, if the boy is a learner, the journeyman is entitled to 5*d*. out of a shilling; that often a master weaver who keeps two looms employed, hath no journeyman but only apprentices, and then a quill-winder, who is hired for 1*s*. 6*d*. per week, will supply both the looms. The reasons why a master weaver has a share so much larger than the journeyman appeared by the same evidence to arise from some few incidental expenses, such as candles in winter time, size, tools, &c. The proportion of the master's net wages to the journeyman's, after all considerations are allowed for and expenses paid, is upon the average of the trade as 7*s*. to 5*s*., or thereabouts."

After hearing the evidence on both sides, the Justices decided "that it was the opinion of every gentleman upon the bench that no equitable rate for settling such wages could be made by any law then in being." Although this narrative was written in the interests of the clothiers, it appears to be a trustworthy analysis of the evidence actually given before the Justices of the Peace. It will be noticed that the Gloucestershire woollen trade was still a purely domestic industry, and that Kay's flying-shuttle had been adopted. The want of employment, of which the weavers complained, was probably due to this invention, for by the old process a wide cloth required two weavers to one loom, which could now be managed by one man. Kay's shuttle, therefore, increased the earnings of the weavers who could obtain regular employment, but many journeymen were probably thrown out of work. The account says nothing of the application of Whyatt's spinning-frame, which superseded the spinning-wheel, and deprived women of an occupation which up to this time had been carried on in their homes. The reduction of the family earnings on this account must be set against the increased wages of the weavers. But the spinning-frame had probably not been introduced into Gloucestershire in 1756.

George Turner, writing forty years later of the same district, says—"The fine trade is at present at a stand, but the coarse for army clothing and the East India Company is remarkably brisk. The introduction of machinery for every process the wool goes through to the loom, has thrown many hands out of employ; and several gentlemen I have consulted attribute the enormous rise of poor-rates entirely to that cause. These, I have credibly been informed, amount in some instances, in the immediate vicinity of the manufactories, to 6*s*. in the pound and upwards yearly." George Turner is an unsympathetic writer, and greatly exaggerates the wages of the weavers. He ascribes the increase of poverty to "the vicious and profligate habits of the weavers, who can, if good hands, earn a guinea and a half a week, which, supposing the carding and spinning machines to have deprived the women and children entirely of employment, is certainly sufficient, properly laid out, to maintain their families comfortably." We may compare the earnings of the Gloucestershire weavers with those of the cotton "manufacturers" in 1741, when the cotton manufacture was still a domestic industry. The weaving of a piece containing 12 lbs. of 1*s.* 6*d.* weft, a very coarse quality, occupied a weaver's family about fourteen days, and the price for weaving was 18*s.* Spinning the weft cost 9*s.*; and picking, carding, and roving about 8*s.* Spinning and preparing the linen warp cost 18*s.* Thus the total cost of workmanship would be 53*s.* for a piece of coarse cloth weighing about 24 lbs.

§ 17. *Conclusion.*

It is not within the scope of this work to describe the industrial changes which took place at the end of the eighteenth century, and which have extended since that period to nearly every industry. But, on the whole, it is in the highest degree improbable that the industrial system, which has been gradually superseded in the last 150 years, ever had those pleasing characteristics which have been attributed to it. Without minimizing in the slightest degree the evils which unrestricted license enabled employers to inflict on helpless operatives already on the margin of subsistence, it seems evident that the transition between 1791 and 1825, which was most marked in the textile industries, although it did not include all branches, aggravated and brought into stronger relief old abuses which would have continued unchecked if the workers had remained isolated and fettered by obsolete or oppressive restrictions. The factory system gradually gave them back powers which had been in abeyance for two centuries. It made possible new manifestations of that spirit of association which was well-nigh quenched, and in spite of its many deplorable features, it must be considered an upward step in social development. This should be kept in view at the time when the evils incident to rapid industrial change were increased by the exceptionally high prices of provisions and the heavy taxation of the French war. We approach no nearer the solution of social evils by representing history as the deliberate conspiracy of one class against another. Edmund Burke, speaking of a sister country, said—"We cannot bring an indictment against a whole nation." Neither can we bring an indictment against a whole class. Legislation based on class hatreds must inevitably, as in times past, bring upon the State evils worse than those it is meant to remove, because it will not appeal to the feeling and judgment of those on whose co-operation its efficacy depends. We have to reckon with average human nature, and we cannot wait for the millennium before the work of reform is to begin. Any man who sets about it with ordinary tact can count upon much cordial co-operation from all classes in social work, whether it be in investigation or practical effort.

But the discontent of the present day is very real and well-grounded, and is daily becoming more organized. There are no questions of such vital interest to the community as those which deal with the economic relations of its different classes, and we cannot foresee what vast changes will be brought about in the next few years. Some await with fear their future development—scarcely any, without anxiety; their peaceful and enduring settlement depends, not upon the brilliant qualities of a few individuals, but upon the wisdom, the forbearance, and the patience of all. It is easy to draw up statistics to show the improvement in the condition of the lower classes; it is easy to expose the fallacies underlying many of the demands made in their behalf. But the moral factor, so often overlooked by economists, is enough to outweigh all arguments based on such considerations, and it is by no means certain that the gloomy predictions of forty years ago will not be fulfilled. The revolution which has taken place in sentiment and opinion is of greater importance than the mere industrial changes, and lends a force to the discontent of the nineteenth century, which was almost absent in the period which has been reviewed.

Society has broken away from its old moorings. Class barriers formerly impassable have been removed, and people constantly pass up and down. The arguments of the Gloucestershire clothiers in 1756, based on the "due subordination" of one class to another, have no weight in 1891; for the various classes are bound together, not only by equality of political and municipal privileges, but in many instances by ties of blood. It would be very useful if genealogical study prevailed more extensively amongst the middle and working-classes, for it is probable that without much difficulty sufficient evidence could be obtained to put the latter proposition beyond dispute. We have been able to trace the vicissitudes of a tenant-farmer's family for nearly three centuries.[1] Until the end of the eighteenth century the family was stationary, in the same village, tilling the same ground, and living in the same house. Then some members of the family migrate. We can follow them along the old coach-road to their new settlements. One gradually establishes himself as a small farmer in a village not far from his old home. Another goes farther afield, and settles in a semi-manufacturing town; but a migration never takes place without some definite career in view. With the introduction of railways, the migrations are longer. Gradually, the members

[1] *Vide* Appendix III.

of the family have dispersed over many countries, while some have gone to the United States, Australia, and New Zealand. Some have acquired wealth and influence, or have passed into the professions; others have entered on the humdrum life of ordinary commerce, or retail trade; there are weavers and iron-workers, trade unionists and domestic workers; many are found still on the land, as farmers, gamekeepers, or agricultural labourers; of some all traces are lost. These investigations illustrate the influence of the modern system of free enterprise on distinctions of class. Others may perhaps be able to contribute similar evidence. It is a sphere of social investigation which may prove useful. The more carefully we study the history of the past, and trace the constituent elements of society to their sources, the more clearly shall we see the social evils of to-day in their true perspective. That is at any rate a step towards remedying them.

CHAPTER V.

THREE COMMERCIAL TREATIES.

§ 1. *The Methuen Treaty.*

In former chapters we have dealt with some measures which mark the stages in the decadence of the system of monopoly which characterized the Middle Ages, and the gradual substitution of free enterprise. We shall now examine three commercial treaties, which well illustrate the state of public opinion during the eighteenth century of freedom of trade. These are the Methuen Treaty with Portugal in 1703, Clauses 8 and 9 of the Treaty of Utrecht (1713), and Pitt's Commercial Treaty with France in 1786. A comparison of their provisions and of the circumstances in which they were concluded, will bring into clear relief some of the main points in the growth of free trade.

The Methuen Treaty was a bribe offered to Portugal by John Methuen, the English ambassador, to join the Grand Alliance. Political motives prompted the concession of certain commercial advantages if she would do so. But the form which the bribe assumed was due entirely to the prevalence of the mercantile system, which exercised its greatest influence at this time. It is useful to keep in mind the association in time of the greatness of Holland with the growth of the mercantile system, for the spectacle of that country defeating the power of Spain, and rising into a great position amongst the nations of Europe, with none of the ordinary conditions, as then conceived, for such a feat, showed clearly the economic basis of political power. Thus one tendency of the mercantile system—to encourage the growth of wealth with a view to its political results—became more marked, and encouraged that aggressiveness of which we have already seen instances in the disputes with the Dutch at the Spice Islands, and the Navigation Acts. The balance of trade was considered the best economic test of the prosperity of the country, and efforts were made always to keep the balance of exports over imports "favourable." That foreign trade was held to be the most beneficial which brought the greatest amount of bullion in return for our commodities, not because the Mercantilists considered the precious metals as the only form of wealth, but because they over-estimated their importance as a medium of exchange. The theory arose at a time when we had few commodities for export, and some practical reasons might have been urged in its favour when the country was only just developing its internal resources. The modern mechanism of foreign exchange was not developed; communication between one country and another was difficult, even in Europe; each nation was in a high degree independent, isolated from the rest, and self-sufficient. If English merchants desired to obtain the commodities of a country—the Indies, for instance—which would not take theirs in exchange, how should they get them? The practical answer which suggested itself was that they must purchase them with the commodity which was universally accepted. Thus the Mercantilists believed that the more clearly foreign trade resulted in a balance in our favour, the more power we should possess over all other commodities. If there was no such balance, England must rely for her foreign supplies on those countries which would take our commodities in exchange. The theory of the balance of trade was a generalization reached after crude observations of facts, which it must be admitted were likely to mislead rather than suggest the underlying principles of foreign trade. The development of finance, the telegraph and ocean-going steamers, have destroyed the conditions which rendered possible the theory of the balance of trade. So far as it went, it was a sincere and more or less accurate attempt to solve an intricate problem.

There was then a political and an economical element in the mercantile system, of which the Methuen Treaty is a good illustration. The treaty was inspired by jealousy of France, and, strictly adhered to, would diminish her influence by cutting off one fruitful source of wealth, the wine trade with England. It should be pointed out, however, that the Methuen Treaty was to some extent a departure from the principles which had inspired former commercial arrangements between England and Portugal. Charles I. concluded a treaty with John IV. in January 1632, which established freedom of trade and commerce with all the Portuguese possessions in Europe, subject only to the usual customs and duties which were paid by the native merchants. In 1647 free importation of wheat into Portugal was permitted, and in 1654 Cromwell concluded a new commercial treaty, extending the principles of the treaty of 1632 to the Portuguese possessions in the West Indies. A secret article provided that the duties on English goods and merchandise should not be greater than twenty-three per cent. *ad valorem;* and no alteration was to be made but by the consent of two English merchants, dwelling in Portugal, and nominated by the English consul. In 1656 the English in Portugal were exempted from paying *decima* on their stocks, "which all the other dwellers in this kingdom paid"; and in 1668 free importation into Lisbon was permitted of wheat, barley, rye, Indian corn, pulse, flesh meat, cheese and butter, arms, powder, horses, gold and silver in bullion or coin, and books.

The Methuen Treaty was probably suggested by the prohibition of French goods in 1678. Such a treaty was advocated in that year on the ground that the importation of the wines of Portugal would be "of great advantage after the expiration of the said prohibition, because it would be the interest of this nation to spend those wines, which are purchased with our manufacture, before those of France, which are purchased with our money, and the introducing of them in the present conjunction might be a means to bring them into use and expense for ever hereafter." It was also urged that the abatement of the wine duties would probably lead the Portuguese to evade the sumptuary law of the year before, which prohibited the wearing of foreign cloth, gold and silver lace, and other commodities, in order to encourage native manufactures.

The economic principle on which the *British Merchant* justified the treaty, was that we gained a greater balance from Portugal than from any other country whatever. The Portuguese were to admit English cloths and other woollen manufactures, "as they were accustomed till they were prohibited by the laws"—alluding to the prohibition of 1677, when the Portuguese Government prohibited foreign woollen goods in order to encourage their own manufacture. In return for this privilege, and as a condition of it, the wines of Portugal were to be admitted at two-thirds of the duty payable on the wines of France. If this second provision should not at any time be carried into effect, the Portuguese Government might prohibit English woollen manufactures.

§ 2. *Commercial Relations of England and France.*

There was, during the seventeenth century, great jealousy in England of the growing commerce of France, and this became more bitter during Colbert's administration, who, it was believed, would make France the chief market of the world if his designs took effect. This jealousy was of long standing. In 1606 James I. concluded a commercial treaty with Henry IV. of France, but neither country obtained any considerable advantage. The French trade continued to be carried on in accordance with this treaty until 1623, when it was confirmed by Louis XIII. But in 1626 commerce with England was prohibited. Three years later Louis XIII. issued a declaration re-establishing commerce with England, and removing several duties, but the rivalry of the two nations soon found expression in hostile tariffs. In 1632, commerce was again "re-established" by a treaty between Charles I. and Louis XIII., but in 1641 many laws were passed injurious to British trade. Eight years later the Commonwealth prohibited the importation of French wines, wool, and silk, in retaliation for the seizure of the woollen goods of English merchants; but in 1654 a commercial treaty was concluded which removed these hostile regulations, and allowed English merchants to import their woollen and silk manufactures into France. There was a curious provision that cloths ill-made be carried back into England, without paying any duty for them. In 1657 the tax levied on merchants and strangers was remitted, as far as the English were concerned, though the French continued to enforce it on the Netherlanders. But the feeling of English merchants was on the whole hostile to France. "They make store of manufactures in their own countries; they need not ours, or inconsiderable quantities in respect of what we bring from thence do amount to, whereby their nation becometh inrich'd and ours impoverish'd, driving us out of our treasures by degrees, for what answers not our export must be put into those commodities by exchange or in monies." They complained of the competition of Holland in the north of France. Most of the English manufactures of wool were well imitated in France, so that "little or none of ours vents in that kingdom. But our cloth made of Spanish wooll still remains in good demand, and at least 7 parts of 8 of all that is made here is consumed in France." According to the French tariff of 1664, all goods were rated at 5 per cent. *ad valorem*, except the manufactures of silk, gold, silver, hair, thread, and wool, on which there was a duty of 10 per cent. *ad valorem*. Defoe remarks that "this tariff was esteemed by all the nations in these parts of Europe to be very easy, and not the least interruption to their trade with France." These duties were afterwards increased fourfold. In the same manner England endeavoured to prevent the importation of French goods by high duties or total prohibitions.

A great quantity of wine was imported from France, and some people also saw with alarm the increased importation of French brandies, which rose from an inconsiderable quantity in 1668 to 4000 tuns in 1674. Its total prohibition was advocated on the ground that "it would prevent the destruction of his Majesty's subjects, many of whom have been killed by drinking thereof, it not agreeing with their constitutions. How many instances have we had yearly of men's dying suddenly, after drinking of brandy? How many, after over-drinking of themselves with this liquor, have been languishing till they have died thereof?" People used to drink good ale and beer. "But now this sort of people, since brandy is become so common, and sold in every little house, a small quantity costing them 3*d.*, do sometimes spend their day's wages in this sort of liquor before they get home in an evening, and thereby impoverish their families; and not only so, but frequently, by their drinking to excess, they are bereaved of their senses for two or three days together, so that they cannot work. In short, brandy burns the hearts of his Majesty's subjects out."

But it is to be feared that the objection to the importation of French brandy was not generally based on the danger of an excessive use of the stimulant. The principal reason for the hostility of the commercial classes to the trade with France was that the balance was against England, while the high duties imposed on English manufactures brought home to every merchant the disadvantages under which he laboured. In spite of the prevailing jealousy, Charles II., in 1677, concluded a treaty conferring various reciprocal advantages, but the prohibitions were repeated in subsequent years on the ground that "the importing of French wines, etc. hath much exhausted the treasure of this nation, lessened the value of the native commodities and manufactures thereof, greatly impoverished the English artificers and handicrafts, and caused great detriment to this kingdom in general." High duties were afterwards substituted for the absolute prohibition. It was argued against the prohibition of 1678, that it could not much prejudice French trade, for it was the interest of traders to elude it; that prohibitive laws rarely took effect, because of the negligence of the port officials, and the large extent of coast and creeks for clandestine operations; and that if the goods were imported they would certainly be sold without difficulty. But the high duties were partially successful, for the English consumer resorted to the wines of Italy, Spain, and Portugal, and to the linens of Holland and Silesia; and so learnt to do without the commodities of France. This circumstance helped to render ineffectual the negotiations begun in 1697 for a commercial treaty. Possibly also the difficulty was increased by the influence of the French refugees, who fled to England upon the Revocation of the Edict of Nantes, and introduced many skilled trades, notably improvements in silk manufacture. Some of the duties were also appropriated to certain uses—*e.g.*, the payment of interest on the National Debt. Thus the jealousy of France, which suggested the unequal conditions of the Methuen Treaty, was no new sentiment, but one which had already found expression in absolute prohibitions or high tariffs. Moreover, the erroneous theories which inspired that hostility to France commended the treaty to the English commercial classes, for the trade with Portugal left a large balance in favour of England, which was paid in the precious metals. Macpherson naïvely remarks that "it has since been discovered that there may be better branches of European commerce than that of Portugal." But in 1703, and for many years afterwards, the commercial classes regarded the Methuen Treaty as one of the highest achievements of enlightened statesmanship.

The treaty was in the main successful; that is, it inflicted some damage on French commerce at the expense of the English consumer, who paid handsomely for his jealousy of his neighbours, drank smuggled wine, or substituted port for Burgundy. The effect on Portugal was more serious. Capital flowed into the wine trade, to the exclusion of other forms of industrial enterprise, and the Portuguese devoted themselves to vine cultivation for the benefit of their English customers. The result is seen to this day in the backwardness of their manufactures.

§ 3. *The Treaty of Utrecht.*

The Treaty of Commerce with France in 1713 was an attempt at more cordial relations, and, if it could have been carried into effect, it would have been a most important step in the direction of free trade. As early as May 1709, the Commissioners of Trade were requested by the Earl of Sunderland to consider several treaties of commerce with France, and to report which of them was most for the advantage of Great Britain. They communicated with the leading merchants, and prepared a draft of a treaty. In March, 1711, St. John sent them another scheme, which was amended and returned to him in April 1712. When the negotiations for peace were commenced, the English plenipotentiaries were instructed to demand a Treaty of Commerce. There were many difficulties, but ultimately a treaty was negotiated, which showed a great advance on any previous arrangement between France and England. There were forty-one articles relating to commerce and navigation, but the controversy turned on Clauses 8 and 9. These provided (1) that all subjects of Queen Anne and the King of France should enjoy the same commercial privileges as the most favoured nation; (2) that, on the part of England, the duties on French goods should not be greater than the duties on those of any other country, and all prohibitive laws passed since 1664 should be repealed; (3) that, on the part of France, English goods should be rated according to the tariff of 1664, and all laws contrary to that tariff should be repealed; (4) certain goods were excepted. These and other questions raised by England were to be referred to Commissioners, who should meet in London within two months and remove all difficulties. "At the same time, they shall endeavour (which seems very much for the interest of both nations) to have the methods of commerce, on one part and t'other, more thoroughly examined; and to find out, and establish, just and beneficial means on both sides for removing the difficulties in this matter, and for regulating the duties mutually." Meanwhile nothing was to prevent the tariff of 1664 from coming into effect within two months after Parliament passed an Act for that purpose. Other clauses equalized the duties on tobacco imported into France, and removed the taxes on the ships of both countries. Needless to say, this treaty would not bear the test of the later free trade criticism; but these events took place more than sixty years before the *Wealth of Nations* was published, and in tracing the growth of a great movement we must not, at every stage, expect a conformity with the principles which are its consummation. The true significance of the Treaty of 1713 will be seen if it is compared with the Methuen Treaty, which has just been discussed, and Mr. Cobden's Treaty of 1860. In 1703 England obtained certain advantages from Portugal by granting special privileges to that country in its competition with France. In 1713 no such privileges were granted; the treaty simply amounted to this, that each country allowed the other to trade on the conditions which subsisted between itself and other European nations. In 1860, England obtained a reduction of the duties imposed on goods exported to France, on condition that France enjoyed certain advantages which were to be extended to all other nations whatever.

§ 4. *Reception of Free Trade Clauses.*

No sooner were the terms of the treaty made known than a storm of opposition arose in the country. The Tory Government and the majority of the House of Commons at this time appear to have been in favour of free trade, but party feeling combined with the bigotry of the commercial classes to ruin the treaty. Petitions poured into the House of Commons, setting forth the calamities which the 8th and 9th clauses would bring upon the country. London, as was to be expected, was the centre of much opposition. The merchants and manufacturers were practically unanimous in their condemnation of the treaty, and the Levant Company were loud in their complaints of the danger to their monopoly of the importation of raw silk. In London, indeed, the various branches of the silk trade were perhaps the most bitter in their opposition. The silk-weavers maintained that their trade had increased twenty-fold since 1664, and if no provision were made to encourage the English manufacture of silk, thousands of families would be ruined by the French competition. The silk-throwers said that they employed more than 40,000 men, women, and children in London alone, who would be reduced to poverty if the treaty took effect. Those engaged in the woollen manufactures made common cause with the silk-weavers. Many petitions came in from Gloucestershire, Worcestershire, Oxfordshire (Witney and other places), Devon, Somerset, Dorset, Wilts, and Hampshire, foretelling ruin to the woollen trade, increase of paupers, and a fall in the value of lands. Norwich, Colchester, and the Eastern counties joined in the cry. The linen manufacturers of Lancashire said they employed 60,000 persons, and prayed that such duties might be continued upon foreign linen as would give due encouragement to the British manufacture. Liverpool feared that the removal of duties on French brandies would prejudice the plantations and discourage navigation. Whitehaven urged similar objections to the treaty. The manufacturers of Leeds expected a falling off in the Portuguese demand for their woollen goods, and prayed that the duties on Spanish and Portuguese wines might be lowered in proportion to those of France. The sugar-bakers, distillers, etc., of Bristol, Worcestershire, and other districts, foretold the ruin of their trade if French wines and brandies were admitted. Those engaged in the various branches of the iron and hardware manufacture did not take alarm. The struggle was carried on in the House of Commons, and in numerous pamphlets and other publications. Amongst the latter, the *British Merchant*, which expressed the views of the commercial classes, and the *Mercator*, which, under the editorship of Defoe, pleaded for the treaty, were the most remarkable. "When the Bill," writes Bolingbroke to Lord Strafford, "was committed in the House of Commons, Sir Thomas Hanmer and some of our friends below-stairs, Lord Anglesea and some of our friends above-stairs, grew squeamish, and began to think, or to say they thought, that this Bill ought to be put off till next session, because the elections might be prejudiced by passing an Act concerning which the opinions of mankind were divided. The Court were willing to have dropped the Bill, rather than to have made a breach among our friends; but the body of the

Tories absolutely refused to part with it. On Thursday, June 18th, 1713, the debate lasted till eleven at night, when the Bill was lost by 174 against 185. The reason of this majority was that there had been, during two or three days' uncertainty, an opinion spread that the Lord Treasurer gave up the point. If this was intended to hurt the Court, it was no very wise nor grateful part in some people; it will have the contrary effect, for every day the prejudice ceases, and the nation becomes sensible of their true interest." But the Tory Government was never able to renew the project of a treaty with France, and our old relations with that country continued.

§ 5. *Significance of the Controversy.*

We can now draw some general conclusions from this agitation. There was doubtless a small minority of the commercial classes in favour of the treaty; but, generally speaking, they showed a united front in opposition to all advance towards freedom of trade between England and France. The causes are not far to seek. They feared that if the Methuen Treaty were superseded, Portugal would retaliate by prohibiting the importation of English woollen goods, and that French competition would ruin the English silk manufacture. Moreover, the Portugal trade resulted in a large "balance" in favour of England, and the treaty practically proposed to substitute for it a commercial connection with France which, it was said, had always left a balance of nearly £1,500,000 against this country. The treaty, therefore, not only struck a blow at the interests of large manufacturing classes, but ran counter to the most cherished convictions of the commercial world. Defoe, Brown, and the other free trade writers in *Mercator*, devoted themselves to refuting the arguments of the opponents to the treaty. It must be pointed out, however, that they accepted the theory of the balance of trade, although they attempted to prove that the trade with France would be beneficial to this country, whether the balance were favourable or not. They objected to prohibitions and high duties, because, they contended, it was the interest of the country to encourage exportation in every possible way, but they approved in the main of restraints on importation. Their great service consisted in the isolation of economical from political considerations in the discussion of the relations between England and France.

This position is stated in the following passage: "The ambition and greatness of the French king, the differences about religion or civil government, can have no share herein; the power or tyranny, or call it what we please, of the French king, can be no reason why we should not trade with him. No man will say the Pretender is concerned in the affair of commerce; there are no Jacobites in matters of trade: neither will they say that we should decline trade with the French because they are Papists, or that the Ballance of Power is concerned in this thing. The cant of parties is a mere jargon in trade, and has neither argument or sense in it. Trade is no way concerned in such disputes as these; we trade with the bigoted Italians and the stupid Portuguese, the Mahometans in Turkey and Persia, the Barbarians of Africa, the savages of America, the Heathens of China, and in general with everybody and every nation whom we can trade with to advantage. *Trading nations, tho' Christian, ought to maintain Commerce with all People they can get by.* Gain is the desire of merchandize: trade is a commutation of merchantable commodities between one country and another, and for the mutual profit of the traders. The language of nations one to another is, *I let thee gain by me, that I may gain by thee.* . . . Trade is an affair of peace: whatever quarrels there may be between nations, trade is at war with nobody: neither, if men were wise, would they suffer war to interrupt trade upon any account whatsoever; especially if that trade may be carried on to advantage. If we were able to have traded with France all the war to our advantage, and did not do it, by so much we weak'ned ourselves, and assisted the French in fighting with us. . . . Trading is a matter entirely independent in its nature, and neither consults other interests, nor depends on any interests, but what relate to itself. To bar up trade with a nation, because we differ in State matters and Political interests, is the greatest absurdity that a nation can be guilty of."

Nearly fifty years before it had been pointed out how matters likely to advance the material prosperity of the country engrossed the attention of statesmen, and that peaceful foreign relations were necessary for the development of commerce. "Trade is now become the lady, which in this present age is more courted and celebrated than in any former. . . . But war is not the means by which this lady may be won."

It was a great advance to separate the pursuit of trade from the lust for political influence in the balance of Europe. But in the eighteenth century the supremacy of the commercial classes was not favourable to peace, and the endeavour to secure the monopoly of the new markets provoked more bitter feeling and more bloodthirsty wars than the religious dogmas which economical considerations had superseded. During the eighteenth century international relations were largely determined by the commercial ideas of the time. If, in the seventeenth century, trade and commerce were subordinated to political designs, in the eighteenth nations went to war for the sake of a market. It was not until the principles of the *Wealth of Nations* were widely accepted that the nation was prepared to adopt the position of Defoe and the other writers in *Mercator.*

§ 6. *Negotiations with France.*

After the failure of 1713, no attempt was made to establish a free trade with France until 1782, though the French appear to have been anxious to trade with England. Even on mercantile principles it was to their advantage to export to England their linen, silk, and wine. But the old prejudices were losing ground. Amongst English statesmen there was a clearer grasp of the principles of foreign trade before any great change was observable in the pamphlet literature of the subject. Bolingbroke was apparently sincere in his advocacy of free trade. The King's Speech of 1721, inspired by Walpole, contained a remarkable declaration: "We should be extremely wanting to ourselves if we neglected to improve the favourable opportunity given us of extending our commerce, upon which the riches and grandeur of this nation chiefly depend. It is very obvious that nothing would more conduce to the obtaining so public a good than to make the exportation of our own manufactures, and the importation of the commodities used in the manufacturing of them, as practicable and easy as possible." This was not an idle declaration on the part of Walpole, for, as Mr. Lecky points out, he persuaded Parliament in the session of 1721 to remove duties on export from no less than 106 articles of British manufacture, and duties on import from thirty-eight articles of raw material. Shelburne, influenced probably by the Physiocrats, was before his time in his advocacy of free trade, and if he had continued in office he would undoubtedly have anticipated Pitt's commercial treaty with France. Lord North's Irish policy also shows the influence of the new principles. Burke was never in a position to give practical expression to his views. His measures of economic reform in 1780 had little relation to trade and commerce; but Adam Smith said he was the only man he had met who had independently arrived at the principles which he advocated. Pitt's enthusiastic acceptance of the principles of the *Wealth of Nations* is well known. No better illustration could be given of the change in the commercial policy of England at this period than the contrast between Lord Chatham, the last great statesman of the mercantilist school, and his son, the disciple of Adam Smith. "France," said Henry Flood, "the object of every hostile principle in the policy of Lord Chatham, is the *gens amicissima* of his son."

The commercial relations between England and France formed one of the principal subjects of dispute in the negotiations of 1782, at the conclusion of the American war. Vergennes, prompted by Du Pont de Nemours, was no less interested than Lord Shelburne in promoting a free trade between the two countries. The French demanded certain modifications of the Treaty of Paris, chiefly the abandonment of the clause relating to the demolition of the fortifications of Dunkirk, and, in addition to this, the conclusion of a commercial treaty. The Treaty of Versailles, containing this stipulation, was signed in 1783. For the next three years there were many delays, apparently on the part of England, the French demanding the fulfilment of the commercial clauses of the Treaty of Utrecht. English goods forced their way into the French markets in spite of the high duties imposed upon them, and it was no doubt the aim of French policy at this time to secure some counter advantages in the trade with England. They were sincere in their desire for a commercial treaty, and it was probably the hope of hastening the negotiations that they prohibited English imports in 1785. If that was so, they had the satisfaction of obtaining their object, for that measure inflicted great damage on some English industries, and threatened considerable loss of revenue by substituting a clandestine for a legitimate commerce. The English Government awoke to the advantage of the connection with France, and in the spring of 1786 Mr. Eden was sent to Paris to reopen the negotiations for a treaty. The appointment of Mr. Eden was favourably received by the manufacturers. He found the French Government willing to grant every facility in coming to an arrangement. M. de Rayneval, especially, the French commissioner entrusted with the negotiation of the treaty, condemned the system which had hitherto prevailed between the two countries, which in his opinion had tended to encourage contraband trade, to give advantages to neighbouring nations, to maintain an unfriendly disposition between France and England, and to embarrass their commerce and navigation. But for some months there was a suspicion of the real designs of France. Even Pitt declared to Eden that "though in the commercial business he thought there were reasons for believing the French might be sincere, he could not listen without suspicion to their professions of political friendship." There were also many difficulties in conciliating the various trade interests which were involved. George Rose "trembled at the very mention of a repeal of our manufactured silk laws," though he believed the prohibition unwise. In the eyes of the ribbon manufacturers, "anything short of absolute prohibition seemed to involve *them*, and of course *the country*, in immediate ruin and destruction." Eden might well exclaim at the unfairness of demanding the importation of English cottons while French silks were excluded. But the English Government would not give way, and the latter continued to be prohibited. The treaty was signed on September 26th, 1786.

§ 7. *Terms of the Treaty of* 1786.

We will give a brief summary of the provisions of the treaty, pointing out in what respect it differed from the Treaty of Utrecht. Turning first to the staple commodities of France, wines imported directly into Great Britain were to be admitted at the duties hitherto paid by Portugal, but the Irish import duties were to remain at the same level. The English Government reserved the right of making a further arrangement with Portugal, in accordance with the Methuen Treaty of 1703. The duty upon French vinegars was reduced from £65 5*s*. $3\frac{12}{20}$*d*. per tun to 7*s*. per gallon, while olive-oil was to be admitted on the terms granted to the most favoured nation. A great blow was struck at the clandestine trade in French cambrics and lawns by reducing the duty upon those commodities to 5*s*. per demi-piece of $7\frac{3}{4}$ yds., and in return for this concession France agreed to reciprocal duties on linens equal to those of Holland and Flanders. Ireland in this respect again received special treatment; in the linen trade between Ireland and France there were to be reciprocal duties not greater than those on Dutch linens imported into the former country. In the more important branches of English industry great concessions were obtained. The hardware duties were to be classed, and nonc were to exceed 10 per cent. *ad valorem;* while cottons, woollens, and hosiery were to pay 12 per cent. *ad valorem*—those mixed with silk excepted, which remained prohibited. The great advantage of this arrangement, which succeeded a state of absolute prohibition, will be realized if the changes which were revolutionizing the textile manufactures are kept in mind. In the very year of the treaty James Watt brought from France Berthollet's invention for chemical bleaching, which made the process one of a few hours only; while machinery was applied to calico-printing, cylinders with continuous patterns being substituted for the square blocks of wood, from which patterns had hitherto been impressed by hand. The year before had seen the steam-engine of Boulton and Watt. It was nearly twenty years since the invention of Hargreaves' spinning-jenny, seventeen years since Arkwright's water-frame, and thirteen since Hargreaves' invention for machine-combing, afterwards included in a patent by Arkwright, began to threaten with destruction the old method of combing by hand. Three years before the treaty the atmospheric engine had been applied to machinery in Manchester, and now Cartwright, Bell of Glasgow, and others were working towards the power-loom. In spite of the high duties before 1785, the improvements in machinery had enabled English manufacturers to maintain a great export trade with France. If in 1664 a duty of 10 per cent. was felt to be "no great interruption" to trade with France, in the new conditions of 1786 such a tariff was not likely to weigh heavily on English commerce. The principle of reciprocity was adopted in the case of other commodities. Saddlery was to pay 15 per cent. *ad valorem;* millinery, porcelain, earthenware and pottery, plate-glass and glass-ware, 12 per cent.; and gauzes 10 per cent. These duties were not to be altered but by mutual consent, and if additional advantages were granted to other European nations, France and England engaged to allow their subjects to participate in them. Head-money (*argent du chef*), an old tax on merchants levied in various forms, the duties on ships, passports, and other restraints, were abolished. The treaty was to continue in operation for twelve years. The differences between this treaty and that of 1713 lay chiefly in the conditions on which French manufactures were admitted into this country, and it is in this respect that the advance in public opinion is chiefly noticeable. By the Treaty of Utrecht the tariff of 1664 was payable on English goods imported into France; but England, on the other hand, only engaged to repeal such duties and prohibitive laws as had been imposed since that year. Thus the numerous statutes passed before that time, which prohibited woollen goods, saddlery, hardware, etc., would have remained in force. The Treaty of 1786 repealed all these prohibitions, and substituted competition on equal terms, so far as the duties were concerned. Neither of the contracting parties cared much for the interests of the consumer, though Pitt asked the Opposition if it was a serious injury for us to obtain as cheaply as possible the luxuries of France, which our own refinements had converted into necessaries. To admit their wines on easy terms, he thought, would only supplant a useless and pernicious manufacture in this country.

§ 8. *Reception of the Treaty by the Commercial Classes.*

The treaty was not received with that outburst of indignation and alarm which had followed the Treaty of Utrecht; the manufacturers for the most part approved of it. Pitt was able to state that "no great manufacturing body of men had taken the alarm," and that in most parts of the country they looked "with sanguine wishes" to the ratification of the treaty. In four or five months there was only one petition of any importance, and that did not object to the treaty, but asked for further time for consideration. Several causes combined to effect this change in the attitude of the commercial classes. Pitt skilfully avoided the difficulties which wrecked the Treaty of Utrecht. He did not propose to supersede at one stroke that "commercial idol of England," the Methuen Treaty, though the new arrangement with France practically made it a dead letter. Thus he disarmed the opposition of those who clung to the prejudices of the mercantile system. The Portugal trade was sinking into insignificance compared with the other great channels of English commerce, and there were numerous complaints of the non-fulfilment on the part of Portugal of the terms of the treaty. The strongest opposition to the Treaty of Utrecht had come from the silk manufacturers and those indirectly interested in that industry. Pitt kept these people quiet by wisely refraining from interference with existing conditions, a course of action which was certainly justified by the magnitude of the other interests involved, and which had received, in the *Wealth of Nations*, the approval of Adam Smith. He thus calmed the fears of those who might have communicated their alarm to other sections of the commercial world. The manufacturers also with whom Pitt had to deal were of a different type from the merchants and clothiers who flourished under the domestic system, and who sent up their petitions from the quiet country towns in the east and west. The centre of gravity of the textile manufactures was moving northwards, and the factory system of to-day was in its childhood. There was a numerous and growing body of men with great capital and of unbounded energy and enterprise. These men were making the industrial revolution, and some of them were keenly alive to the disadvantages under which they laboured, as long as high duties hampered them at home and foreign markets were closed to them. Already they were agitating for the repeal of the cotton duties, and it was not difficult for Pitt to win them to his side with the glowing picture he drew of the future extension of English commerce. More accurate principles of political economy were also forcing their way. While the *Wealth of Nations* marks an epoch in the development of economic science, it derived much of its influence from the fact that it systematized and brought to a focus ideas which in a confused and incoherent form had been for a long time gradually winning acceptance, and which, with the experience of every year, gathered strength. The conclusion of peace with America marks not only the end of a long struggle with rebellious colonies, but also the destruction of those economical errors which had partly inspired it. The severance of the connection between the colonies and the mother-country was not followed by those disastrous results to English commerce which many of the wisest men anticipated; on the contrary, the substantial advantages of the connection remained, and were every day growing. There were also many men who looked with disapproval on a meddling foreign policy, and hailed with joy the beginning of more friendly relations with France. Wilberforce expressed their views when he stated that the manufacturers were favourable to the treaty, attacked the theory of the balance of power and interference in European politics, and pointed to the national debt which adhesion to that theory had occasioned. In addition to these various influences tending to modify public opinion, the manufacturers were conscious that they had nothing to fear from French competition.

"I was very intimate," writes a Glasgow manufacturer, "with old Holker at Rouen; the first time he showed me his works was in a forenoon, when he boasted much of the cheapness of wages; after dinner, when men are more open, he told me that though he had a pension of 12,000 livres, and many indulgences and exemptions from the French Government, he could not make his cotton goods so cheap as he had done in England. I asked how his conversation after dinner agreed with his conversation before it. His answer was that they were very consistent, that he gave cheap wages, but got little work, for that a French artisan lost his time in twenty little pleasures which an Englishman had no notion of, such as dressing his hair a full half an hour every day, making love, walking with the women, dancing, sitting long at table, going to mass, chatting with his companions, etc.; and he added that I would find every article in France (millinery goods alone excepted) dearer than in England. . . . The price of cotton goods depends now a good deal upon machinery, where we have a solid superiority over the French from the cheapness of our coal, by which the steam-engine is directed, and which steam-engine has an hundred advantages over works conducted by wind or water. This last observation ensures us in the superiority of woollen—for although Mr. Arkwright has as yet applied his machine only to cotton, yet there can be little doubt that it will be equally applied to woollen. . . . With regard to wines and brandies, the powers of chemistry are running so rapid a progress that France will not get the benefit there which she expects. . . . I remember the time when cambrics were much cheaper at Glasgow than in France, and when everybody wore them, and the Glasgow people went out of the business only because printed linens at one time, and the gauzes and lawns at another time, and the cotton at the present time, are a more profitable article. Whenever these fail them, they will return to the cambrics again. I can tell you a curious anecdote which will show you the facility with which these transitions are made. Mr. John Cross had a great rope-works at Glasgow; he quarrelled with his men about wages, and about thirty of them left him. He did not mind it much at first, supposing they would come back again; but seeing nothing of them for some weeks, he inquired after them, and found they were all sitting on fine lawn looms at Paisley. With regard to millinery, the French will ever possess it, as long as their gentlewomen amuse themselves with working in nunneries, instead of going about to speak ill of one another."

§ 9. *Debates in the House of Commons.*

The keenest opposition to the treaty found expression in the House of Commons, where Pitt had arrayed against him Fox, Burke, Sheridan, Philip Francis, and Henry Flood. The last-mentioned was a thorough-going mercantilist of the old school, and he eloquently denounced Pitt's departure from his father's principles. The others allowed party considerations to override their judgment. Possibly Burke's experience with his Bristol constituents made him more cautious in the application of the principles which he had more than once professed. He had great difficulty in opposing a treaty which must on the whole have met with his approval. He complained that Pitt, "with that narrowness which led men of limited minds to look at great objects in a confined point of view, regarded the treaty, and wished it to be regarded, as a mere commercial consideration." He appealed to the old prejudices about the Portugal trade, pointed to the danger of French competition, and threw doubt on the real designs of France in promoting the treaty. Fox never had any economical principles. The treaty appeared to him the beginning of a "new system, in which not only the established doctrines of our forefathers were departed from, but by which the great and most essential principles in our commerce, principles which, whether wise or erroneous, had made us opulent, were to be completely changed. . . . He was not convinced that it would be wise for England to enter into a commercial connection with France, unless it was clearly demonstrated that such a connection was in no wise to affect our valuable connection with Portugal. . . . The Methuen Treaty had justly been considered as the commercial idol of England." "France was the inveterate and unalterable political enemy of Great Britain. No ties of affection or mutual interest could possibly eradicate what was so deeply rooted in her constitution." Pitt had the support of Grenville, Dundas, Wilberforce, and, in the House of Lords, Lord Lansdowne (Shelburne). The ease with which the treaty was carried through its principal stages is an indication of the change which had taken place in public opinion. The commercial classes saw the advantage of an extended market for English goods, and the Opposition had no support in the country. As far as they were concerned, the tide was turning in favour of free trade. Their interest lay in the removal of restrictions. The free trade movement of the nineteenth century assumed a new phase, when the interests of the landlords and farmers began to be attacked. They occupied the position of uncompromising hostility, which in the earlier stages of the movement had been filled by the commercial classes.

§ 10. *French Views of the Treaty.*

The French manufacturers were disappointed with the results of the treaty. They, for the most part, condemned it altogether, or represented that the advantages derived from it consisted only in the substitution of a legitimate commerce for the clandestine trade which had formerly been carried on. According to Arthur Young, the Birmingham manufacturers were also of this opinion. At Abbeville, Amiens and Lille, Young found the most violent opposition to the treaty, and the Lyons manufacturers resented the exclusion of silk. At Bordeaux, however, it was considered "a wise measure that tended equally to the benefit of both countries." Young tells an amusing anecdote of his visit to the fair of Guibray in August 1778: "I found the quantity of English goods considerable, hard and queen's-ware; cloths and cottons. A dozen of common plain plates, three livres and four livres for a French imitation, but much worse. I asked the man (a Frenchman) if the treaty of commerce would not be very injurious with such a difference. 'C'est précisement le contraire, Monsieur. Quelque mauvaise que soit cette imitation, on n'a encore rien fait d'aussi bien en France;

l'année prochaine on fera mieux ; nous perfectionnerons : et enfin nous l'emporterons sur vous.'" The Chamber of Commerce of Normandy, in a pamphlet based on the inquiries of two Rouen merchants, regarded the treaty with strong disapproval on the ground that various French manufactures, especially those of cotton goods, pottery, and coarse woollen goods, could not withstand English competition. They asserted that the treaty had not been followed by an increased trade, and that this was especially the case with French wines. They maintained that the terms of the treaty favoured England at the expense of France, and that these conditions united with the Navigation Act to cause a great disproportion in the number of French and English vessels engaged in the commerce of the two nations. Monsieur Du Pont de Nemours, who had inspired the treaty, replied to the objections of the Normandy Chamber of Commerce. He pointed out that their information with regard to the wine trade was inexact; and that, as a matter of fact, the City of London alone, in the last eight months of 1787, had imported four times more wine than the three kingdoms had done before in a whole year. While he admitted that English competition might be mischievous in some branches of French manufacture, he attributed the decline of the Lyons silk industry, not to the treaty of commerce, but to the successful exertions of Spain for improving the fabrics of that country and to the failure of the crop of silk. He examined the course of exchange with England before and subsequent to the treaty, and showed that the balance of trade was in favour of France.

§ 11. *Conclusion.*

There can be no doubt that the treaty contributed to the great prosperity which marked the early years of Pitt's administration. In his unrivalled Budget Speech of 1792, in which he dwelt on the vast and growing resources of the country, and pointed to the improvement in social welfare which might be expected from the increasing accumulation of capital, he looked forward to many years of undisturbed peace, during which his reforms might be perfected. He welcomed the great changes which were revolutionizing and extending the commerce of England into every corner of the globe, and foretold, "in spite of the vicissitudes of fortune, and the disasters of empires, a continued course of successive improvement in the general order of the world." "The scene which we are now contemplating is not the transient effect of accident, not the short-lived prosperity of a day, but the genuine and natural result of regular and permanent causes. The season of our severe trial is at an end, and we are at length relieved, not only from the dejection and gloom which, a few years since, hung over the country, but from the doubt and uncertainty which, even for a considerable time after our prospect had begun to brighten, still mingled with the hopes and expectations of the public."

In the following year we became involved in a long and expensive war, and the movement, whose initial stages have been described, was checked for forty years. The reforms, which it was hoped would be the commencement of a career of unbounded progress, served only to increase the stability of the country in its struggle with revolutionary France. It was not until the appearance of Huskisson that the movement of the end of the eighteenth century was given a new life.

The period which has elapsed since his accession to office in 1823 is one of the most remarkable in English history; and the labours of Peel, Cobden, Bright, and Gladstone, who followed him, will never be forgotten. Until 1842 the movement was hampered by the difficulty of repealing taxes without detriment to the public services; the revival of the income-tax by Sir Robert Peel supplied the necessary means for overcoming that difficulty, and the next ten years saw the repeal of the corn laws, the abolition of export duties, of import duties on raw material, and of certain oppressive excise duties. Mr. Gladstone, strengthening his position by pressing into his service other aids, like the extension of the succession duty to real and settled property, cleared the way for further reforms, and the movement was carried to its completion. A firm believer in the doctrines of Adam Smith, there is scarcely room for doubt that William Pitt would have anticipated many of the free trade measures of later years, if it had been his lot to enjoy ten more years of peaceful administration. There are many points of resemblance between the Treaty of 1786, his greatest measure, and the Treaty of Commerce with France negotiated in 1860 by Richard Cobden. No man before his time, and no man since, with one exception, has possessed in such a high degree that powerful imagination which can penetrate to the deep social and moral significance of the dull details of commerce and finance, combined with statesmanship of the highest order. It is idle to speculate what might have been the future of England if there had been no French war, no period of reaction in England, and if William Pitt had presided, during a long life engaged in peaceful reforms, over the transition from the old order to the new.

APPENDIX I.

WEAVING, BY THE PIECE.

1583—1698.

RATES QUOTED FROM THOROLD ROGERS' 'AGRICULTURE AND PRICES.'

Date.	Description of Weaving.	Place.	Rate.	Date.
1583	Canvas	Gawthorp	85 yds. @ 5*s.* 42 yds. @ 3*s.* 4*d.*	1583
1586	Blanket	,,	44 yds. @ ¾*d.* yd.	1586
1587	Cloth and Linen	Worksop	1*d.* & 3*d.* yd.	1587
1588	Canvas	Gawthorp	½*d.* ¾*d.* & 2*d.* yd.	1588
	Blanket	Worksop	1½*d.* yd.	
1589	Frysado	,,	1*d.* yd.	1589
1590	Cloth	Gawthorp	1½*d.* & 1*d.* yd.	1590
	Linen	,,	1*d.* yd.	
	Woollen	Worksop	34 yds. @ 3*s.*	
1591	Hempen	Gawthorp	80 yds. @ 1*s.*	1591
1594	Canvas	,,	1½*d.* yd.	1594
	Fine shirt linen	,,	6*d.* yd.	
1595	Hempen and Flaxen	,,	168 yds. @ 11*s.*	1595
	Not stated	Worksop	46 yds. @ 2*s.* 2*d.*	
1596	Canvas	Gawthorp	105 yds. @ 5*s.* 10*d.*	1596
1597	Shirting	,,	4*d.* yd.	1597
1598	Canvas	,,	25 yds. @ 1*s.* 3*d.*	1598
1607	Cloth	Theydon Gurdon	4*d.* yd.	1607
1608	,,	,, ,,	2¼*d.* yd.	1608
1609	Canvas	Gawthorp	1*d.* yd.	1609
1616	Blankets	,,	7 st. @ 2*s.*	1616
	Towen napkins	Theydon Gurdon	2*s.* 6*d.* doz.	
1618	Cloth	,, ,,	19 ells @ 5*d.*	1618
1619	Napkins	,, ,,	2 doz. @ 3*s.*	1619
1620	Towcloth	,, ,,	20 ells @ 2*d.*	1620
1621	Woollen cloth	,, ,,	12½ yds. @ 2*d.*	1621
1623	Napkins	,, ,,	2 doz. @ 6*s.*	1623
1698	Sheets	London	3*s.* 9*d.* pair	1698
	Narrow cloth	,,	36 ells @ 3½*d.*	

APPENDIX II.

RATES OF WAGES

TO BE PAID TO THE

WOOLLEN BROAD-CLOTH WEAVERS.

GLOUCESTERSHIRE QUARTER SESSIONS, 1727.

Hundreds of Threads.	Rate per yard.
	d.
400 to 500	3
500 ,, 600	4
600 ,, 700	4½
700 ,, 800	5¼
800 ,, 900	6
900 ,, 1000	6½
1000 ,, 1100	7¼
1100 ,, 1200	8
1200 ,, 1300	9¼
1300 ,, 1400	10½
1400 ,, 1500	12
1500 ,, 1600	13¼
1600 ,, 1700	14½
1700 ,, 1800	16
1800 ,, 1900	17¼
1900 ,, 2000	20
2000 ,, 2100	21½
2100 ,, 2200	24

APPENDIX III.

NOTE ON THE HISTORY OF THE FAMILY AND DESCENDANTS OF A TENANT FARMER.

THE following remarks, vague as they must be, may be found useful in illustration of pages 127, 128. The family apparently remained stationary in the same district, probably in the same village, for several centuries. It is difficult, almost impossible, to obtain reliable information on such a subject before the beginning of the seventeenth century. There is good reason, however, for believing that representatives of this family may have been found, engaged in agriculture, in the same village from the beginning of the fourteenth century onwards. From the beginning of the seventeenth century till the present time there seems to have been no break in the continuity of their residence in this village. Certain information can be obtained after the middle of the eighteenth century. M and N, husband and wife, had a large family, all of whom could not be supported by their parents as they grew up, or obtain employment in their native village. Some of them migrated into the villages in the immediate neighbourhood, where they obtained employment on farms or engaged in trade. Some of their descendants are still in the district, employed in agriculture or market gardening, or combining retail trade with the latter. I do not know what other changes have taken place in these younger branches of the family.

The eldest son of M and N was twice married. By his first wife he had three sons—A, B, and C. After her death, probably in the year 1800, the father married again. The disagreeable treatment which the boys received from their step-mother, combined perhaps with the difficulty of obtaining employment, caused them to seek their fortunes elsewhere. It is not clear, but it is probable that all three had some definite position in view when they left home. We find them employed on farms in a village fifteen miles away along the high-road. The eldest, however, A, did not rest here, but pushed on some miles further, to a village in the neighbourhood of a small town engaged in textile manufactures. His eldest son A^1_1 was apprenticed to a weaver, and became a prominent trade unionist in the district. He died a few years ago. B remained in the village where he had first found employment, and ultimately developed into farmer and bailiff. He had two sons and one daughter. The eldest son B^1_1, still alive, is a small farmer in the same district. He is assisted by his son B^2_1, who himself has a young family. Two other sons, B^2_2 and B^2_3, have migrated, the one to Warwickshire, the other to South Wales, but I do not know their present employment. The second son B^1_2 was also a farmer, but he died some time ago. His children have left the district. One of them became a gamekeeper on an estate some miles away, and has a young family. The others I have not yet traced, except so far as to discover their whereabouts. The daughter of B, B^1_3, is unmarried, and I believe lives by glove-making. C very soon left the village he reached after first leaving home, and obtained a situation (exact nature unknown) on a farm near a manufacturing town, P—, fifty miles away. This was the longest migration hitherto in the history of the family. He remained in this position, married, and had one son, who found employment in one of the iron-works in the district. Upon C's death in 1831, A migrated with his family, and succeeded him in his position. By this time A's first wife had died, and he had married a second time. He had a numerous family. The eldest A^1_1 has already been mentioned. I have not yet traced his children. None of A's children remained where their father lived. His eldest daughter, A^1_2, married, and went to live in a north-midland town. Of her children, some emigrated to Australia, where a numerous colony of them may be found. They are, I believe, woollen merchants. The other children of A^1_2 are engaged in business — photography—in their native town. They have numerous families. The younger children of A first found employment near home, some in the iron-works in the district and others in business. Of their descendants the more successful may be found in various trades and professions. The less successful have gradually deteriorated under the hard conditions in which they earned their living. Generally speaking, I should say that in the history of this family agricultural surroundings have proved favourable, not only to physical vigour and length of life, but also to some of the more important elements of social and moral well-being. Agricultural life does not offer many methods of advancement, but the qualities of a good farmer or an efficient labourer on a farm are rare and difficult to acquire. In the history of this family there are no instances of the possession of these qualities in a high degree.

The influence of town conditions seems to have been felt in the following ways—

(1) They have widened the area of choice of a means of livelihood. It is unusual for the son to follow the calling of his father in the new conditions.

(2) Comparing those engaged in agriculture with those living in town conditions, the change appears to have shortened the length of life, but I refrain from expressing a final opinion on this point until the members of the family have been more completely traced.

(3) One thing, however, is clear. The new conditions have stimulated the more vigorous members of the family, who have taken advantage of the many opportunities which town life affords of improving their position and prospects. But the weaker members have gone to the wall.

I defer further remarks until I have finished the investigation of this family (1) by more carefully tracing it in the male line, and (2) adding particulars from the examination of the female line. I hope also to be in a position to give particulars of at least two more families.

INDEX.

Richard Clay & Sons, Limited, London & Bungay.

www.ingramcontent.com/pod-product-compliance
Lightning Source LLC
Chambersburg PA
CBHW030830270326
41928CB00007B/976